IRacing Paddock

- Beginner's Guide to Road Racing on iRacing.com -

By

R Bryden

©2010

- *Dedicated to Mimi, Cristiano and Alessandra for their boundless patience and understanding... for which I shall be eternally grateful*

- *And also to my late father and brother, John Joe and Bernie, who fostered my passion for racing and are both dearly missed*

Foreword

The reception afforded iRacing.com has been a source of great pride and satisfaction to everyone on our team since we first offered our online racing service to the public in 2008. Although confident iRacing.com would be accepted within the sim racing community, we also hoped to introduce online racing to whole new audiences of "real world" racers and motorsports fans. So we're delighted that many, many people with little or no sim racing experience have joined our service and are now enjoying the opportunity to race in the virtual world.

Online racing is challenging, rewarding and, above all, fun. But newcomers to the sport face a steep learning curve, not just with respect to race driving and car set-up, but in terms of selecting the hardware, software and computer systems -- as well as arranging the appropriate environment – to maximize their enjoyment. Recognizing this, we developed the iRacing.com Quick Start and User Guides, along with the iRacing.com Sporting Code, to make beginners' initial experiences with our service as enjoyable and pain-less as possible.

However, an additional perspective on the basics of iRacing is invaluable. That's why I'm delighted that Ray Bryden, one our most enthusiastic and knowledgeable members, has taken the time and made the effort to develop the *iRacing Paddock*. In it you'll find all the fundamentals of iRacing explained in a systematic, detailed and common sense manner, with a dash or two of Ray's good humor. It's an excellent companion to the official iRacing documents and one that is sure to enhance your online racing experience.

So read it, learn from it and enjoy it. Most of all, welcome to iRacing.

Dave Kaemmer

CEO and CTO, iRacing.com Motorsports Simulations

All rights reserved. No part of this publication may be reproduced, stored in a retrieval system, or transmitted in any form or by any means without the prior written consent of the copyright holder.

Author's Cataloging-in-Publication Data

Bryden, R

    iRacing Paddock / R Bryden with a Foreword by Dave Kaemmer
    Includes Index.
    p. cm.
    Language: English
    ISBN: 145154667X
    EAN-13: 9781451546675
    Primary category: Sports & Recreation / Motorsports
    Published in the United States

Copyright © 2010   R Bryden

ISBN 145154667X

Table of Contents

Foreword iii
Introduction viii
The Basics of iRacing 1
Simulator Hardware 2
    Computer Hardware 2
    Computer Elements 3
    Extra Hardware 11
    Environment and Ergonomics 15
Driving 20
    Rookie Resources 20
    Driving Hints 23
Racing 33
    Read and Understand the Sporting Code 33
    Set Your Goals 33
    Preparing 34
    Practice Offline (Testing) 36
    Practice Online 36
    Time Trial 37
    Qualify 37
    Preparing to Race 38
    The Race 40
    Post-Race 47
    Debrief 48
    Statistics 49
    Protesting 49
iRacing.com™ Car Specifications 51
    Pontiac Solstice (Rookie Class) 52
    Spec Racer Ford 57
    Skip Barber F 2000 62
    VW Jetta TDi 67
    Car Setup Guide 72
    Car Comparison 75
iRacing.com™ Track Content 76
    Lime Rock Park 77
    Mazda Raceway Laguna Seca 81
    Summit Point Raceway – Main Course 85
    Summit Point Raceway – Short Course 89
    Summit Point Raceway – Jefferson Circuit 91
    Charlotte Motor Speedway – Road Course 94
    Charlotte Motor Speedway – Infield Road Course 98
    Centripetal Circuit 100
FIRST Official Sporting Code – Version 2010.1.15.01 101
Index 129
Final Thoughts 131

Special Note

Since I am not an iRacing employee, opinions in this book are my own, and do not reflect the views of anyone in that company. Moreover, the advice given is only given for guidance, and certainly other viewpoints (friends, other iRacers, online reviews, etc.) are valid and should be sought out. I received no suggestions about what to include and what to cover – anything not included is simply an oversight and not meant to favor one item over another (thinking mostly about hardware). And since I obviously have not tried every possible piece of hardware, it is not my intention to favor one over another in any case.

Beyond the *Official User Guide*, the *Quick Start Guide* and the iRacing FAQ and knowledge base, there are plenty of resources available to ask for further advice, starting with the iRacing forums. I highly recommend new users make use of the forums, and in particular, one should be sure to check out the club forum on the main iRacing forum site, as there are plenty of people (some may live very close by) who are more than willing to help with any questions or problems.

All screenshots and logos along with track descriptions and a copy of the FIRST Sporting Code from iRacing.com are used with permission. iRacing and iRacing.com are trademarks of iRacing.com Motorsport Simulations, LLC (Bedford, MA).

Thank You's

Special thanks to the staff of iRacing for their software which I genuinely enjoy, and obviously led me to write this book. Particular thanks to Dave Kaemmer and John Henry for bringing their vision into reality for all of us. Thanks also for iRacing's assistance in getting some of the pieces of the puzzle in place. Thanks especially to David Phillips for looking it over and finding a myriad of grammatical errors and suggesting fixes for my sometimes clumsy wording.

I also thank the many dozens of iRacing subscribers (too many to name) who have helped me along in my early days to figure out what I was doing wrong, or providing some insight about setups or other iRacing intangibles. I also want to give thanks to those who have helped to grow the sim racing and iRacing community with websites, internet media telecasts, or general helpfulness on the forums.

Most of all I thank my family for allowing me this indulgence and for fostering my racing passion all these years.

Introduction

This book is intended to guide beginners and newcomers to the iRacing service in the basics of computer and sim-racing hardware as well as providing some general guidance on driving the beginner level cars – specifically the Pontiac Solstice, the Spec Racer Ford, the Skip Barber F2000, and the VW Jetta TDi. In addition, there are lots of details about the road courses included with the subscription, and finally a copy of the Sporting Code at the end.

The goal is to familiarize the user with the evolving sport of sim-racing, particularly with regard to the premiere online environment for sim-racing at iRacing.com. There are many pitfalls for a new sim racer or even one with experience who is new to iRacing, and my hope is that this book will serve as both a guide for setting up the service as well as a handy reference when trying to find ways to improve.

Experienced users may also find some of the vehicle data and track specific information and track maps of value in optimizing setups and working on trouble spots, since most drivers can find improvements if they look hard enough. I believe there is also plenty of content here for die-hard oval racers to use in terms of computer hardware and race preparation which are universal in sim racing.

I hope you enjoy your time at iRacing and feel free to pass along any feedback to me by private message via the iRacing forums.

The Basics of iRacing

This book will not include details about installing the software and learning the very basic functions and how to get things going for the simple reason that it has already been laid out in detail by iRacing. There are three important resources listed below that one must use to learn how to install and use the software's basic functionality and solve any basic problems you may encounter. If you have problems that are not solved using these resources, send an email to support@iracing.com.

Quick Start Guide

This is probably the most important resource for new users as it guides you through the basic steps in getting the software installed and also explains many of the fundamentals of the service such as how to navigate the website and join an event, as well as basic explanations of the different sessions and the importance and principles of the Safety Rating and iRating systems. Taking a few minutes to review this guide is essential to learn the basics of iRacing.

http://members.iracing.com/membersite/member/instruction/qsg_10.jsp
(link also available on the main iRacing member page under "Reference")

Official User Guide

Again, this is essential for new users as it provides important details about all aspects of controls and options and functionality which are not covered in the *Quick Start Guide*. This includes everything from modifying your user account settings to explanations of saving and editing replays. To avoid the frustration of trial-and-error experiments when learning how to set things up the way you want them, spend time to go through the User Guide.

As a side note, an important section of the *Official User Guide* is the 'On Track Controls' section. The most useful of those is the F3 information display which shows the drivers nearest you and the approximate time gap. This is particularly important when exiting the pits – one should avoid jumping out onto the track from the pits when a driver is approaching at full speed. Time your exit so as to not cause an accident or frustration among your fellow drivers.

http://membersmedia.iracing.com/pdfs/20100212_UserGuide.pdf
(link also available on the main iRacing member page under "Reference")

iRacing Frequently Asked Questions (FAQ)

In writing this book, I had intended to include a comprehensive FAQ to cover many of the questions new users frequently have, but then I realized it would be a wasted effort since a comprehensive iRacing FAQ and knowledge base already exists. IRacing maintains the web-based FAQ to answer many recurring questions from users, particularly with regard to troubleshooting technical problems or other unexpected occurrences. New users should bookmark the site to refer to as the first step when questions or problems arise.

http://www.answers-script.com/iracing/index.php

Simulator Hardware

Racing Computer Setup

In order to race safely, you need to have a system capable of keeping up with the needs of the simulator. Just because your computer can handle an empty track doesn't guarantee that a full grid of cars won't hobble your frame rates to slide-show speed. Some people are surprised to find as a large field of cars dives into turn one at the start that their normally fast and stable system suddenly becomes undriveable for a period of time, particularly if there are some incidents going on.

Computer Hardware

Any mention of hardware in this book does not constitute an endorsement or absolute recommendation. Ask others sim racers for recommendations if you are not sure, and rely heavily on online reviews of products you intend to purchase.

Pre-Assembled Systems vs. Pick and Choose

Many computer vendors offer pre-assembled systems which are tempting for users with limited hardware skills or knowledge. This is a great solution if you have more money to spend and especially if the vendor offers some selection to components, particularly if they pre-test the system to ensure everything works.

However, many will find that with a small investment of time and effort, they can save several hundreds of dollars by selecting components themselves and assembling the system at home. Most computer components are now pretty easy to assemble and putting a computer together from scratch is not something to be feared. It is probably no more difficult than putting together a desk from IKEA.

The key is to select the right components you will need and buying from vendors with great support should something go wrong. A computer can be put together from its component parts in about an hour (probably less than 15 minutes for someone with experience), but installing the operating system and other needed software (e.g. antivirus) can take several hours.

Consult manuals, online help sites or ask a friend with good computer skills for advice or help if you need it. Posting an ad on a high-school bulletin board can provide you with an excellent IT support person for very little cost.

Vendors

There are hundreds of reputable computer vendors. You can avoid potential problems by researching vendors on Google's shopping site or rating sites like resellerratings.com or even asking advice from other iRacing members about ones about unfamiliar vendors. Look into their return policy and be aware of any restrictions. There are at least two companies, Main Performance PC (http://mainperformancepc.com/) and A Unique Computer (http://www.auniquecomputer.com/), run by iRacing members who create systems specifically tailored to run iRacing.

Buying on eBay is a great way to save a lot of money, but you have to be able to trust that you will get what you expect, and if not you should be aware of the seller's return or support policy. Let the buyer beware! Most eBay or classified ad items will not come with a warranty unless otherwise stated.

Computer Elements

Monitor

CRTs are a thing of the past, but will still work if that is what you have. However, if you are buying a new monitor, LCD panels are your only realistic option. Some good quality monitors >20" are available for $100-150, while some larger than 27" can be found in the $300 range. Some people decide to use TV's as the monitor which can be a third option. Again, look for advice from fellow sim-racers or online reviews.

If you have the budget and space, a larger monitor is obviously preferred as it will allow you to see more of the track and people racing alongside. You will need to find the best field of view (FOV) setting in the game to allow you to see enough of the peripheral action without the dash and forward view looking too distant.

Some users enjoy an expanded FOV by using 3 monitors to view more of the side angles. The expanded canvas allows drivers to see into the turns much better and allows for a much more immersive experience. In addition, it allows drivers to see other cars alongside to a much greater degree, which can make side-by-side racing much safer, particularly for oval racing.

A free utility called SoftTH is the lowest cost option for multiple monitor setups. However, those that have used the hardware option known as TH2GO (~$300), say that it is a much better solution (easier to set-up and use). The TH2GO limitation is that it only works with specific monitors (capable of 57Hz refresh rates), which could be a limiting factor if you already have monitors available which don't meet the requirements. Another option has become available known as "ATI Eyefinity®" which is available on new generation cards from ATI. The main limitation is having to use at least one monitor which includes a DisplayPort input option or using an active DisplayPort adaptor which sells for about $100 US.

Graphics card

Although some people can race with laptops, it is generally not a great option due to the limited graphics capabilities (in all but the high end gaming laptops). Desktop graphics cards fall into two basic flavors: ATI and nVidia. Until recently, most computer gurus claim that nVidia cards had the edge in performance, but it depends on how much you are willing to spend. The newest ATI 58xx may have shifted the balance toward ATI, at least for the time being. But the high-end video card market changes quickly. Highest end cards fall in the $200-400 range which will allow for maximum eye-candy (off-track objects and higher resolution textures) and in the case of ATI, the potential for three-screen setups as described above. Mid range cards at $100-200 offer the best compromise in terms of performance and cost, while value cards ($25-100) can handle basic graphics but will not offer a combination of high frame rates and eye-candy.

I opted for the mid-range with an ATI 4830/512 Mb. My ASUS motherboard offered Crossfire X support (allowing use of multiple GPUs), and since it came with an on-board ATI GPU, I am now running both GPUs in Crossfire mode. However, it doesn't appear to have improved my frame rates (and may have actually dropped it a little). Other people claim good success with higher frame rates when using multiple graphics cards running under Crossfire (ATI) or SLI (nVidia).

Although some argue that eye-candy is unnecessary in racing, I believe having more off- track objects helps to give more braking point markers and visual reference targets to keep you consistent from lap-to-lap.

ATI: *http://www.amd.com/us/products/Pages/graphics.aspx*
nVidia: *http://www.nvidia.com/page/home.html*

CPU

IRacing suggests users have a dual core processor at a minimum. This is due to the fact that one processor is assigned most of the physics calculations while the other processor handles all the rest. I opted for a triple core CPU (AMD 8450) and found that one core shoulders the workload (to about 50% of maximum usage), while the other two were about 15-20% utilized. The third core in this case was likely assigned normal background tasks. I doubt a fourth core in a quad-core CPU would have any usage at all. In the future, iRacing intends to off-load some functions (such as sound) to other cores beyond the primary two, which would make having three or four cores more of an advantage. In my case, based on the performance I am getting and looking at the CPU load and temperature, I doubt having a faster CPU would gain very much in terms of system performance.

CPU selection boils down to Intel or AMD. In the past, AMD was seen as the better value (lower cost for equivalent level of performance), but the balance has shifted to equal or slightly better performance per dollar for Intel systems. However, for the purposes of iRacing systems, CPUs from either manufacturer will be more than appropriate.

http://www.amd.com/us/products/Pages/processors.aspx
http://www.intel.com/products/processor/index.htm

RAM

For RAM, more is typically better until you exceed 3 GB in a 32-bit system (above this would be unused). Although 64-bit systems can use more RAM (up to 16.8 TB!), iRacing is a 32-bit application and is limited to addressing 3 GB, so having more than 4 GB available is of debatable use. However, RAM speed will have an impact on performance and thus faster RAM will always be preferred. Opting for a motherboard capable of using faster bus and RAM speeds is advisable. However, one should take to ensure heat will not be a problem (faster speeds generate more heat), and that the system can be stable when under stress. A program known as 'memtest' can verify if the RAM has any stability problems.

http://www.memtest.org/

Motherboard

Select a motherboard with a good reputation for quality. ASUS, MSI, and many others have an excellent track record of quality motherboards with a stellar reputation for support including downloadable BIOS updates and system drivers.

If you intend to run multiple monitors (like a 3 monitor setup), it may be useful to pick a motherboard with a built in GPU as it will have the needed video output in case your graphics cards don't have the needed number of outputs. Having multiple PCI slots for adding video cards later for more graphics power is another feature many look for.

Other things to look for are support for faster processors and RAM speeds, should you choose to upgrade at a later time. Other included features such as several USB ports, a LAN port, and other input/output ports will often come in handy. Be aware of all the connectors available on the motherboard in case you intend to use existing components. In my case, I purchased a motherboard with only one IDE port (for a hard disk) and thus could not utilize my IDE DVD burner.

Case and Power Supply

The best system is one that is operationally stable and cool. Tuck away loose wires from the power supply or use rubber bands to keep them out of the way. Install enough case fans to keep a healthy supply of air running through, and try to keep the area dust free. Regular cleaning of the components and motherboard with (e.g. with a careful blast of compressed air or using a small vacuum tool) will help optimize cooling.

If you have many open slots, configure the cards on the motherboard so that they are not close together. Remove unused hardware which can drain the system of power or clutter the case making cooling more difficult.

Proper cooling is essential in keeping a stable, trouble- free racing system. The best location for such a system would be in a cool room away from other heat sources, such as a basement. My system is in an unheated room adjacent to the basement room where my cockpit is located. Short wires for peripherals and a wireless keyboard/touchpad are all that is needed to keep the fan noise from the cockpit, and keep the room heat from the computer. I also wired up a remote switch to turn on or reset the computer.

When choosing a case, opt for a larger one with ample room for movement of air, which also allows for easier maintenance (cleaning) and upgrading components.

The power supply should have ample power to sustain all the hardware in the case, along with any peripherals using system power (for example, through USB ports). High performance video cards are a large drain on the power and now often require a special power connection to the power supply, whereas in the past all the power was taken from the motherboard.

I recommend purchasing a power supply well above the recommended limits of your current video card. At some point you will want to upgrade your video card or add a second card to your system, and if your existing power supply cannot handle the extra power requirements, you will need to upgrade it as well. So try to buy a much more powerful power supply than you will think you will need. If your card recommends 400W, buy a minimum of 550W, or preferably more. Keep in mind that the CPU/RAM, hard disks, DVD drives, audio card, and unpowered USB peripherals all will drain power from the power supply – often simultaneously, so having a larger overhead of available power is strongly recommended.

Audio

Audio is an often overlooked aspect of computer performance, and users generally make use of the sound processor included with their motherboard. When using this approach in Windows XP, I had some occasional lock-ups while iRacing which did not appear to be heat related, but I suspected were linked to an audio conflict of some kind. By installing an old sound card I had lying around, the lock-up problem disappeared.

If the core which processes sound has lots of room for more resources, you can change the number of sounds processed by editing the "numSoundStreams" in the iRacing/app.ini file. Default is 16 (range = 12 – 63), but you can go higher for better sound if your system can handle it (make sure to leave enough headroom for extra CPU power when needed, otherwise you can have bad stuttering problems (low frame rates). The same option can be lowered when your system has a slower CPU and can thus help when running in a large pack of cars near the start of a race when frame rates drop dramatically.

Speakers

Speakers should be placed to enhance the stereo sound. Speakers built into monitors will work, but the sound is typically very low quality and is not recommended. Even modest speakers will offer a much richer experience, and a subwoofer (preferably placed behind your back or under your seat) will go a long way in making the sound of the engines come alive.

Headset

Headphones are obviously important where loud sounds could disturb others. Be careful not to use too much volume as long races with a loud engine noise pumped into your ears can damage your hearing.

You may find that using speakers and headphones together will allow for better communication, since the spotter and voice-chat can be fed to a different sound output (e.g. a second sound card), enabling you to hear the engine noise from the speakers and the voices from the headphones. In this case, open ear headsets would be preferred, in order to hear the sound from the speakers.

Another alternative for spotter prompts and voice chat would be to use a USB Bluetooth adapter and connect to a Bluetooth earpiece (cell phone headset) to allow for a lightweight option which includes a microphone.

Microphone

Many users enjoy using microphones to communicate with other drivers during online sessions. Testing the mic by joining a populated practice session and asking others if they can hear you is advisable to be sure it is working as you expect.

Keyboard, Mouse

This is pretty basic. Many people are usually close enough to their computer to use a wired keyboard, although some enjoy the freedom of having a wireless mouse and keyboard. Running out of battery while getting ready to race could be a problem, but is easily remedied with a supply of batteries standing by.

I use a wireless keyboard with a built-in touchpad, so I have no need of a mouse. Since it is Bluetooth it can operate well even though the receiver is in the adjacent room, and it includes a recharging station (the keyboard can go for months between recharging). I sometimes have a wired keyboard hooked up and ready to go in the unlikely event that my battery runs out unexpectedly.

Another option is to use a trackball or stand-alone touchpad for mouse functionality, especially when space is limited. Others recommend special gaming keyboards with many programmable keys to allow for faster communication or setting changes by setting up keys or macros. One example is the G15 keyboard from Logitech.

http://www.logitech.com/index.cfm/keyboards/keyboard/devices/3498&cl=US,EN

Operating System

Many users swear by Windows XP, while others claim great experiences with Windows Vista, and now a large portion of the population are experiencing good results with Windows 7. I have used all three without any issues. For Windows 7 I decided to try the 64-bit version (Windows 7 Release Candidate) which opens up more RAM (32-bit systems are limited to about 3 GB of RAM). So far my 4 GB RAM + 512 MB video card run smoothly and I have not experienced problems of any kind. The OS automatically found all the required drivers for my system and installed them without any problems.

Some users make use of utilities or manually reconfigure their system to limit the number of modules and background programs installed during boot-up to maximize gaming performance. This is a good option where the system is having trouble keeping good frame rates, and the computer is not used for other activities. When the system is shared with other users or for other activities, separate boot-up sequences can be set-up to run a special gaming set-up when needed without limiting the functionality of the system when used for conventional purposes. A good resource for knowing which programs and operating system modules can be disabled is Black Viper

http://www.blackviper.com/

Drivers

Not sim drivers, drivers that enable your computer to use all the components reliably. Many annoying problems can be solved by driver updates, since many users encounter the same problems and report them to the manufacturers who find solutions and offer updated drivers on their website.

The most important driver updates are usually for graphics cards, as this is a complex part of the system and requires an optimized driver set to function at its best. If the system appears to be running stable it may not be worth experimenting with new drivers, but if you need a performance boost, or to attempt to solve an annoying hardware glitch, it is worth looking into driver upgrades. Read the associated release notes with the driver to see if it should solve any issue you may have been encountering. Also keep your old drivers archived somewhere in case the updated drivers cause problems.

Network Hardware

Modems and routers are an integral part of the virtual sim, providing your track location at every instant and letting you know the location of other competitors at the same instant. A broadband connection is a requirement for iRacing, though there have been a few users with some success using dial-up, or using wireless connections through cell phone providers.

There is probably not much advantage to DSL over cable, though it is often up for debate. A good way to test your connection is to use sites like SpeedTest (*http://www.speedtest.net/*). Satellite broadband is not appropriate for sim racing due to the high latency of the signal connection.

Mostly it boils down to how many routers have to handle your signal before it gets to the racing server. The time required to make that trip is known as the latency or ping time (measured in milliseconds). Enjoyable online races are possible with drivers having less than, say, 150 ms ping time. Higher pings mean there is a delay between where a driver is on the track and where he appears to be to other competitors. To account for this lag, the iRacing system uses a prediction code to compensate where the high ping driver should be according to their position and trajectory data up to that point.

An even more important factor is the quality of the connection, since lost packets of data result in the server having to guess where the driver could be on the track, sometimes with disastrous results for other competitors. With a poor connection, the car will appear to blink (disappear momentarily) to other drivers - to the driver with the poor connection, everyone will appear to blink. Should the poor connection continue for a period of time the server will normally disconnect the driver.

Often this signal disruption can be caused by sharing the network resources with others using connected computers on the same hub. Some routers come with QoS (quality of signal) settings which force one port to have priority over others. Gaming routers are specifically designed to optimize this feature.

Many people are forced to use wireless for various reasons, although they may find higher latency, or lower quality of signal, depending on the local radio interference. In general a wired connection to the router is greatly preferred to maximize the speed and quality of the network connection, which is essential to sim racing.

Wheel, pedals

The most popular wheel on iRacing appears to be the G25 by Logitech which was recently replaced by a similar model called the G27 (~$250-300) which includes a three-pedal set. A lower cost alternative which is also highly rated is the Driving Force GT, also by Logitech ($100-120). The main difference in the two in terms of features is a slightly higher quality pedal set – including a clutch – and an H- pattern shifter for the G25/G27. Many other wheel options from ECCI, Fanatec, Frex, TSW, etc. offer high quality driving sim hardware.

Force Feedback (FFB) is featured on most wheels. While most claim it does not make you faster, it is generally agreed that FFB can help you to feel when you are losing grip and thus offers you better control resulting in fewer accidents. There is also a consensus that iRacing implementation of FFB is among the best on any racing sim.

Look for advice on FFB settings specific to your wheel, should the default setting not be to your liking. I had to dial back the strength settings to be able to feel the feedback without having to fight the wheel through every turn and bump. This can be accomplished in the sim options page, as well as the wheel utility program that comes with most wheels (or can be downloaded from the manufacturer).

Most wheels include a set of pedals. Higher end models usually include a clutch. Since the sim includes an auto- clutch option, and transmission and clutch damage is not currently modeled, the necessity of having a clutch pedal is based only on driver preference.

Pedals can also be purchased separately from various vendors. The most popular at this time remains CST pedals which are sturdy, and hand-built by Todd Cannon (he also offers DIY plans, should you be mechanically inclined).

Fanatec sells a popular three-pedal set known as ClubSport pedals ($199 US). The brake in this set uses a load cell instead of a more common potentiometer configuration. This makes it feel more like a real brake as the response is a function of force applied to the pedal, rather than pedal travel (distance). I have this set myself and have noticed an improvement in my braking feel by using the load cell brake.

http://www.logitech.com/index.cfm/gaming/wheels/&cl=us,en
http://www.fanatec.de/
http://www.cannonsimulationtechnologies.com/
http://thomas-superwheel.com/tswsite/
http://www.brdsim.com/product/controls/pro-st.html
http://www.frex.com/gp/
http://ecci6000.com/

Extra Hardware

Bodnar Components

Leo Bodnar manufactures several components by hand which are valuable to sim racers. The key one is a pedal interface that provides much higher (4x) precision than the normal 0 - 1024 from standard pedals. Some argue that you cannot feel that fine of a difference in pedal resolution; however, some also argue that the benefit also lies in having an input channel separate from the wheel, which reduces input lag. Whatever the reason, most users claim excellent results and satisfaction with Bodnar adaptors.

http://www.leobodnar.com/

Brake Modifications

Most pedal systems packaged with wheels use springs for resistance, and rely upon travel of the pedal to simulate the brake force. In most cars, it is not so much the travel of the brake pedal as the force applied to it which is translated to braking force.

Most spring systems are considered to be too soft and are augmented by various modifications ranging from extra or stiffer springs, rubber or sponge materials behind the pedal to add resistance (the so-called 'Nixim mod', squash ball, etc.).

http://www.nixim.com/cart/index.php?act=viewCat&catId=2

A very popular modification is to replace the brake potentiometer with a load cell. As mentioned previously, this will directly convert force applied to the brake pedal into braking force input for the sim. Some pedals offer this as an option (CST pedals), or can be applied to existing pedals as a DIY project. This would require extra hardware to operate the load cell as a USB input, such as a Leo Bodnar USB gaming interface module (BU0836).

http://www.apelectrix.com/

Gearshift and Clutch

There are a number of H-pattern and sequential shifters in the market and many are included with several wheels. For instance the Logitech G25 comes with a separate shifter which can e configured as a sequential or H shifter with a selector switch. The newer Logitech G27 wheel shifter only operates as an H-pattern shifter, however.

Originally, H shifters offered a slight advantage in shifting time, but that advantage has now been addressed and there appears to be no advantage for any particular shifting hardware type. Many prefer the paddle shift option available on most wheels, since you don't need to let go of the wheel. However, those who enjoy realism often choose to mimic the shifting behavior of the car they are driving with the same equipment in their virtual environment. It is a matter of taste.

Keep in mind that (at least at this point), transmission and clutch damage is not currently part of the sim, and so use of the clutch is optional. A strong contingent of the iRacing population continue to ask for this damage to be instituted for the sake of realism and ensuring proper race driving technique, while others believe that the important thing is just to work the sim the way it is configured and enjoy racing, regardless of the amount of realism, since there can never be a perfect match between real life and virtual racing. There has been recent news that transmission and brake damage modeling will be upgraded soon.

Button box

Bodnar also offers an input module (BU0836) which accepts inputs from potentiometers, as well as switches. This means you could create your own "button box" with a variety of switches for many different inputs for the sim (radio, re- mapped function keys, volume controls, etc.).

An alternative approach would be to find a cheap USB gamepad and rewire the buttons to switches on a button box. This would require a little soldering skill compared to the simple terminal connections afforded by the Bodnar unit.

Shift Light Indicator (SLI)

A shift light indicator is a dashboard or steering wheel add on which includes multiple LEDs to display a linear RPM gauge, indicating to the driver when an upshift is optimal. This could be particularly useful for hearing impaired iRacers who may find it difficult to watch the tachometer and still focus on driving the track. The best known SLI module available which is iRacing compatible, includes a gear indicator LED digit, and is available from Leo Bodnar and CST.

Leo Bodnar (*http://www.leobodnar.com/products/SLI-M/*)
CST (*http://www.cannonsimulationtechnologies.com/new- page.htm*)

3D

Special LCD shutter glasses are available with some support hardware to allow games to provide a true 3-D experience. I tried such a system in a racing sim using a 60 Hz monitor and though the 3-D was good, it did not draw me in like I expected, despite the fact I spent time trying to optimize the system. After about 10 minutes of use it's time for a break as it reliably produces a headache.

Newer 120 Hz monitors are thought to be an ideal answer to this issue, since each eye would receive its own 60 Hz view, like with most current monitors. It is likely that such a feature would require a very high-end graphics card (or cards) to draw different images at 120 frames per second. As a result, there is not much experience in 3-D for the simple reason of the economics of getting a 120 Hz monitor and top of the line video card(s), coupled with cost of the 3-D accessories.

But it is not far-fetched to think that this may be commonplace in the near future.

Multiple Monitor Setups

As mentioned in the section on monitors, a three monitor setup allows a driver to see extra view space by employing monitors to the left and right of the main screen. Thus a much wider field of view is possible. An excellent resource for multiple monitor advice is available on WidescreenGaming forums.
http://www.widescreengamingforum.com/

Once enabled, such systems provide a great function in allowing a much more immersive racing environment, along with an enhanced feeling of speed. Finally, the extra wide field of view is advantageous when battling with drivers who are alongside, so you have a better understanding of where the other cars are in relation to yours.

TH2GO

TH2GO TripleHead is a unit that processes video output from a graphics card to divide into three separate monitor outputs, and is one popular way of achieving this dramatic panoramic display. The disadvantage is the extra cost (~$300) plus the fact that it is only compatible with certain monitors capable of 57 Hz refresh rates. In addition, the monitors should be identical.

http://www.matrox.com/graphics/en/products/gxm/th2go/

ATI Eyefinity

The recently released Radeon 5xxx video card family from ATI offers built-in multiple-screen functionality. The main limitation is having to use a least one monitor having a DisplayPort input, which is currently a rare input feature, and is only available on a few select monitors, such as the Dell P2310H.

http://www.amd.com/us/products/desktop/graphics/ati-radeon-hd-5000/Pages/ati-radeon-hd-5000.aspx

SoftTH

A third alternative with many resolution options and no refresh rate constraint is a free utility known as SoftTH. This creates a single frame panoramic view and splits it into separate monitor outputs to achieve the same functionality as the TH2GO system. The main disadvantage is the difficulty in getting the system set up and optimized, and often requires hours to set up as well as frequent reliance on others online who can assist with setup of SoftTH.

http://www.kegetys.net/SoftTH/

Head Tracking

Head tracking uses a special camera and IR LEDs arrayed on a fixture which can be mounted on a headset or cap. The camera tracks the position of the LEDs and translates that into real time coordinates with 6 degrees of freedom (DOF) including x, y, z, yaw, pitch, and roll.

This technology was originally aimed at flight simulators to provide sim pilots the capability to shift their views with coordinated head movements. There was a natural adaptation to racing simulators, with the key advantages being that the driver can look toward the apex, and also that they can glance beside the car to watch for other drivers fighting for position beside them.

There are currently two main options for head tracking. The first is a commercially available unit for $120 called TrackIR 4.

The second, called FreeTrack, is a free software utility which requires you to use a suitable webcam or Wii remote (which is actually an IR tracking camera), and a DIY LED headset array.

Both operate equally well, however, many who try head tracking are not able to adapt to the new way of seeing the track and having the view move independently of the car. As a result, they struggle to hit their marks and frequently spin or otherwise lose control. On the other, a large number of users adapt well to the head tracking system, to the point that they do not perform as well when it is not used. The only way to know for sure is to try it. The FreeTrack system is fairly easy to configure - the most difficult aspect is putting the 3 LEDs and associated frame and power source together.

TrackIR (*http://www.naturalpoint.com/trackir/*)
FreeTrack (*http://www.free-track.net/english/*)

Buttkicker

Buttkicker provides low frequency vibrations directly to your seat. Instead of subwoofers which transmit low frequency vibrations through the air as sound, the buttkicker system is a direct mechanical vibration of the user via a unit attached to the seat powered by an external amplifier and controlled by sound inputs from the computer. Users report great immersion and enjoyment of the sim when using the buttkicker to augment the feel of a racecar. The latest model (Buttkicker 2) includes an improved amplifier.

http://www.thebuttkicker.com/

Motion Cockpit

There are a wide variety of do-it-yourself, as well as low- and high-end motion simulator cockpits on the market. A DIY system would require a fairly high degree of skill to assemble and optimize, while turnkey systems are much more expensive (ranging from ~$2,000 up to $20,000 or more). Most users have found a greater feel of immersion into the game when feeling the pitch and roll of the car as well as vibrations from hitting the curb. Some even provide yaw capability. The monitor is part of the moving frame and thus the whole system generally requires a robust energy source to move driver, cockpit seat and frame as well as the monitor(s). CXC, however, move the driver in more subtle ways, including actuators which attach to the back of the cockpit seat to provide the motion.

Some examples of motion cockpit vendors are:
BlueTiger (*http://www.bluetiger.com/*)
CXC Motion Simulators (*http://www.cxcsimulations.com/*)
Force Dynamics (*http://www.force-dynamics.com/*)
SimCraft (*http://www.simcraft.com/star.html*)

Environment and Ergonomics

Room Characteristics

Noise
Noise levels work both ways. If you're running at high volume with a subwoofer and at high RPM, you will make a lot of enemies in your house and with neighbors. Similarly, they may find it necessary to raise their voices or TV volume to be heard, which is a serious distraction from driving.

The best compromise is to find a place which is secluded enough to allow you to run the speakers at a reasonable volume without disturbing anyone. If such a scenario is not possible, the next best solution is to use a headset, which will avoid any noise pollution to yourself and others in the area.

Visual distractions
Keeping your monitor against a wall and away from windows or doors, will help prevent any sudden visual distractions which could spell disaster on the virtual track. The best location would be in a quiet corner away from distractions.

Space
This is another area of compromise with your housemates. You will need enough room to incorporate the tools of your hobby (a desk with wheel and pedals, up to a fully equipped cockpit), and this could be a troublesome compromise if there is no spare room to be found. In this case, a portable or easily dismantled system is an option, but the best solution is to work out some understanding with those you live with.

In particular, you should have enough room to be comfortable when racing, and have a setup which allows you to maintain identical posture from session to session. Clutter around a racing desk could be a real problem, particularly if you are bumping into things while trying to steer.

Seclusion
Aside from the previously detailed needs of a quiet and calm environment, having it stay that way during a race or TT session can be a challenge. Having a door to ensure seclusion would be a great asset.

Light level
The worst lighting situation would be having to deal with variable high intensity light, such as glare from the sun poking through trees. Shades on the windows are important to avoid losing visual clarity of the track.

Many find florescent lighting to be a little hard to deal with due to a subtle flicker, the color of the light, or any associated noise. In any event, glare from lights should be minimized to have the best sim experience. Dimmable lights offer a wonderful option to enable you to see your keyboard keys or other nearby objects, without producing distracting glare spots on the screen.

Monitor brightness is another important consideration. The monitor I currently use (28" Hanns-G LCD) is known for its extreme brightness on default settings, and although I was aware of this and turned it down when first setting it up, I found myself dealing with eyestrain after a couple of days of use. I cut the brightness level down to a much greater degree and the eyestrain problem went away.

Temperature and humidity

The last aspect of your sim environment is temperature and humidity control. For driver comfort, this is obviously an important consideration, but it may also play an important role in computer performance, since most systems require large volumes of cool air to keep CPU, GPU and RAM performance stable. On a hot day, the cooling fans may not be enough to draw away the excess heat and you may end up with a sudden shutdown at best, or a fried expensive computer component at worst - particularly if you try to squeeze the most performance out of the computer by overclocking.

Moreover, voltage spikes from the sudden on/off of an air conditioning or space heater may harm sensitive computer components. Isolating the computer system as much as possible or investing in a line conditioner or surge protector could help to save a lot of money when unstable power is a known issue.

Cockpit Designs

Many serious sim racers do well on a simple table or desk setup and find no need to invest in a sim cockpit. However, for those with the space and money, a sim cockpit can offer some convenience and utility.

There is a plethora of different user-bred designs shown on various sim forums, and many of the people who designed and built their own are happy to share their designs and advice with others.

http://members.iracing.com/iforum/thread.jspa?threadID=6262

In addition, there are many companies offering manufactured cockpit setups at prices ranging from one hundred to several thousand dollars. Top of the line motion cockpits can cost as much a low level racecars. However, the sense of immersion some of these machines can offer is of value to many who pursue such high end equipment.

Stationary cockpits by several manufacturers including Obutto, Playseats, Fanatec (Rennsport), and Xlerator offer ready-to assemble cockpits at reasonable prices.

http://www.obutto.com
http://www.playseasts.com
http://www.fanatec.de
http://www.xwstands.com

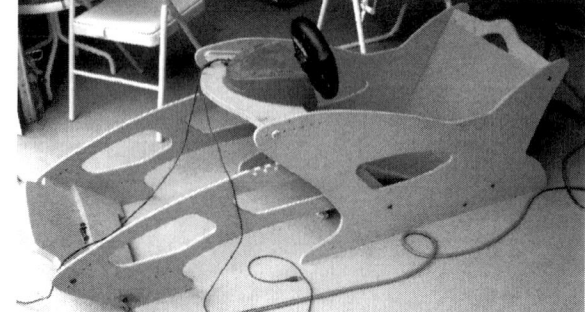

Plans for do-it-yourself wooden cockpits as pictured here are available from various places. This design is the Microsim MK II Racebase whose plans and fittings can be found at thewayiplay.com website:

http://www.thewayiplay.com/mainforum/index.php?topic=894.0

In short, a sim cockpit is not a necessity, but a sign of a big commitment by the sim racer to devote a special space to their hobby. As such, careful attention must be paid to several aspects of the design and the space which it will occupy.

Cockpit Fit and Function

Stability

The cockpit I built out of wood is heavy and sturdy, however, in its original form it was - despite all the glue and screws - quite creaky and unstable. This was cured by stripping down many of the unnecessary panels and superfluous wood (to take away weight), and adding some bolts to secure parts which would normally be free to flex. As a result, the system is now free of creaks and wobbles.

The wheel mount should be as stable as possible and the platform on which the pedals are mounted should also be firm and free from travel during use.

Getting in and out

I liked many of the home-grown designs I saw on the sim message boards, but I disliked the thought of having to crawl into the tight and awkward space (similar to most single seater racecars). My original design had a door and a retractable platform for the wheel, so I could easily get in and out of the cockpit.

As mentioned previously, I stripped down much of the excess weight from the cockpit for stability. This meant no more door, which made access even easier (and now from either side), and the retractable platform remains. This is not ideal as the platform has a little bit of movement possible, but this is lessened to a degree with a simple hook to hold it in place when driving. A simple clamp would work even better.

Seat

The seat, above all else, needs to be comfortable. You can spend a lot of money getting a real race seat for your cockpit, but if you end up with chronic back pain after hours of daily use, then it has to go.

I had a friend buy a plastic racing seat from a swap meet for $10, and it is plenty comfortable during long sessions. Many people incorporate bucket seats from cars (obtained at minimal cost from junkyards). This is a great option, not only for the comfort it provides during long hours of use, but because it also usually includes the mounting hardware which allows for seat adjustments to enable each user to optimize their driving position.

Footwear

The majority of sim racers race in sock-feet, though some are more comfortable in light shoes or barefoot. Specially made footwear for sim-racing known as "Simboots" are available from *www.simboot.com*. Some will put a sock over a particularly abrasive pedal to avoid calluses. Consider also the base of the foot, since prolonged resting of the heel on a hard pedal base may cause some foot pain.

Driving Position

It is critical point to be aware of any discomfort and address any problems you notice as soon as possible, since you can cause a lot of long-term pain from improper driving position, and repetitive strain related injuries.

Knee pain

My original cockpit design had my feet up high and my toes extended when hard on the gas or brake pedal. I did not notice this as a problem when I was driving, but during long races, or practices I would notice a pain in my right knee. Clearly my legs were not operating in a natural position. I then adjusted the pedal height and distance so that it was a more natural position for my legs, and I have not had a recurrence of the pain.

Wrists and fingers - wheel configuration

Driving with a tight grip on the wheel is a bad habit and should be avoided. A firm grasp is appropriate but prolonged use of the wheel with an excessively tight grip on the wheel will result in numbness or 'pins and needles' feeling which is an obvious sign that you are doing something wrong.

The wheel position needs to be optimized for your body size and mechanics, not to mention preference. I prefer having the wheel much closer than others, to the point that my elbows are at my sides. I find this gives me the best combination of precise control and comfort.

Driving schools often prescribe a driving position which includes having your wrists resting at the top of the wheel when you are seated with your shoulders back against the seat. But inevitably, drivers will prescribe their own optimal driving position that suits their body and driving style. Finding the best position for your wheel is an important aspect of your cockpit design. Having flexibility of wheel positioning would be a great asset in the cockpit design.

Keyboard, mouse placement

Many drivers make use of text messaging to other drivers during sessions (more during practice or before or after a race), and having a good location for the keyboard and mouse are important considerations. An adjustable, angled platform is an ideal solution, particularly if you intend to use the keyboard while driving. If keyboard use is limited to before and after sessions (my case), then having a nearby shelf is all that is required. If space is limited, a trackball or touchpad could be a good alternative to a mouse.

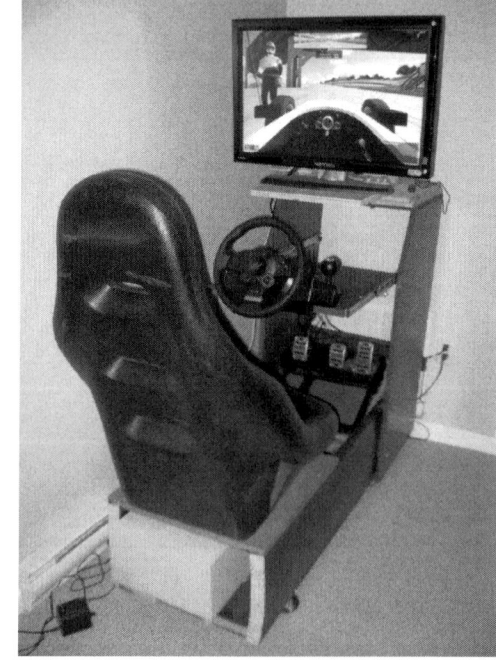

Elbow room

Sitting comfortably in your racing setting is one thing, but keep in mind it is a dynamic environment, and at times you will be doing emergency maneuvers such as a quick 180+ degree snap of the steering wheel or jumping onto the brakes. If the quarters are tight, the odds of bumping into something and doing some bodily damage are high. Try to keep a buffer zone around you to allow for free movement without the danger of breaking some fingers if your hand slips off the wheel during a spin recovery move.

Sharp edges or protruding metal (bolts or screw heads) of cockpit elements should be filed down or recessed when possible, and if your wheel or pedals need modification to adjust to your needs, seek advice from others on sim forums. Often something simple like racquet tape can improve feel on a wheel, or take away an uncomfortable seam which can lead to blisters.

Loose items on cockpit

Pay attention also to items in contact with your cockpit. It can be distracting to have a CD tower land on your lap during a race! How much worse to have a tall beverage glass teetering on your desk that gets knocked over by a missed gear shift and either lands on you, or worse your motherboard. I have experienced several instances where something like small headphones or a desktop speaker have landed on the floor during some aggressive moves, and those events can be quite disconcerting particularly during a wheel-to-wheel battle. A wobbly monitor is even more of a disaster waiting to happen. If the necessary elements cannot be firmly screwed into place, do everything possible to provide as much stability to the system as possible and keep and clutter or unnecessary equipment away.

In another instance I had a full glass of water next to my wheel. At some point during a practice session I felt a drip on my thigh and realized that the aggressive steering was splashing the water from the cup which was ending up dripping from the base of the wheel. Not a severe, problem, but another unnecessary distraction which would have been much worse had it been a race.

Access to items

There are some things you will need to access occasionally. For instance, a reference book (like this one?), or headphones or other accessories. These are best kept nearby but not on or in the cockpit itself, in order to avoid clutter or having wires get tangled in your brake pedal or gearshift. A nearby shelf, bookcase, or night stand are good options for setting down a beverage in a safe place.

Some recommend having a beer-fridge next to the cockpit for easy access to refreshments. But I think occasionally getting up to retrieve these items is advisable. You need to get the blood moving and give your eyes a break occasionally.

Static charge

My plastic racing seat is fairly comfortable on its own, but during the dry winters it can result in a lot of static when I move around on the seat, resulting in mini-zaps. This can be annoying, but also a danger to small electronics that you touch as you build-up charge.

An easy solution for me was to use a throw blanket over the seat (traditional seat covers wouldn't fit), and that resolved the issue.

Storing and Moving

When designing my cockpit I decided that I needed something that could be moved around if needed, so I originally designed it as four separate pieces – the seat, the base, the body shell (mostly cosmetic), and the monitor/wheel stand.

I later removed the body shell to make it lighter and more stable, and added some bolts to hold the monitor stand firmly to the base, which also added stability. The system can be dismantled in a few minutes and be carried (clumsily) around the house. For a recent sim-party I moved it from the basement to the garage in a matter of minutes. By far, the longest part of the relocation is the computer and peripherals setup.

Some prefer portability for storage purposes so it can be out of the way until needed. Usually a lighter frame system such as an Obutto frame or the MK II Racebase cockpits would be advisable for this circumstance.

Driving

Rookie Resources

Starting out in iRacing requires patience and a desire to want to improve your skills as a sim driver and racer. There are several tools which are available to rookies to help quickly learn proper technique and thus compete sooner with more experienced drivers. Some of those tools are discussed below.

Telemetry options

In the near future iRacing intends to add telemetry and split time functionality to the sim. Until then, some user-created options exist such as iSpeed which allows for split times and other live telemetry data on a separate window or screen (screen overlays of the full-screen iRacing window using DirectX have been disabled due to security and cheating concerns).

http://www.nessoft.com/ispeed/

Alternatively, one can enable data-logging of car data using Martine Wedlake's 'vbox' tool which creates a data file which can be read by a freely available viewer from Driftbox.

http://members.iracing.com/iforum/servlet/JiveServlet/download/40-19717-242859-8859/vbox1_4.zip
http://www.driftbox.com/dlsoftware.html

These are valuable tools in learning how to improve your approach to different tracks and shaving precious time from the clock.

If you want to dig deeper into the field of racecar data analysis, look into reading "Data Power" by Buddy Fey (1993) and "Analysis Techniques for Racecar Data Acquisition" by Jorge Segers (2008). And check out their blogs:

http://buddyfey.blogspot.com/
http://sites.google.com/site/jorgesegers2/

Setup sites

Aside from the iRacing forums, there are several internet sites that maintain a database of user uploaded setups for various car and track combinations. An incomplete list is provided here:

http://www.teamdraft.net/Setups.php
http://iracerstuff.com/setups/
http://www.iracersresource.com/
http://forum.racedepartment.com/iracing-setups/
http://www.setup-guru.com/iracing/
http://www.teamredline.co.uk/setups/
http://orionraceteam.com/setups/

Keep in mind that there is no magic setup that will work well for everyone, as car behavior is a function of the setup along with driving style, and so a setup that works well for one person may be inappropriate for another. Over time you may find a driver who provides setups that fit very well to your specific driving style, and thus it is a good strategy to employ their setups wherever possible to get predictable car behavior.

In addition, it is helpful to know that many of the fast road course drivers on iRacing use left foot braking and apply what some consider to be copious amounts of throttle under braking to get a real-time brake bias adjustment. As a result, those drivers tend to use a lot more rear brake bias than one which is optimized for someone not using so much (or any) throttle while braking.

Keep this in mind when trying out setups, as it may need to be tailored to your driving technique. Ideally, the front tires should lock up just before the rear tires. Otherwise, the car could snap into a spin if the rear tires lock up (and thus lose traction) first.

Track guides, videos

Some users also create track guide and instructional videos and replays to show proper line and braking points, along with suggestions for gear selection and other track specific advice.
Youtube is a good source to search for some of these videos. On the iRacing forums you can find links to Robert Björkman's series of instructive videos for driving rookie cars at some of the tracks.

http://members.iracing.com/iforum/thread.jspa?threadID=13174

Driver training is set to be released in iRacing in the near future and will provide video tutorials and instruction on proper technique.

Forums, chat, e-mail

Inevitably, new drivers have countless questions about sim racing and iRacing.com in particular. Many of the problems encountered have been dealt with by others who can provide fast and helpful advice on the forums. Anyone who provides an earnest question can expect a fast and helpful reply. However, as with any internet forums, there is often a tendency for innocent posts to occasionally flare up into an argument. If one does develop, the best strategy is not to reply. Differences can also be settled by a private message email which is found inside the iRacing forums. Be sure to check for messages occasionally.

In online sessions, practice in particular, make use of the chat function (voice or text) when you need help with something sim-related. You will often find a sympathetic and helpful reply instantaneously. Please avoid asking questions while drivers are racing or qualifying as it is considered distracting and bad etiquette.

Expert Hints

This book is intended to give rookies some advice on getting up to speed with the sim a little faster and avoiding some common pitfalls. For specific driving instruction there are several options available. As mentioned above, the iRacing driver training modules are due to arrive soon. Absent these training modules, you can ask for help from others in the forums or in online sessions; next I would seek out renowned books which provide expert advice for drivers looking to improve. The best text for novice drivers is Going Faster which has a wealth of knowledge and advice for controlling a race car and maximizing performance. Next would be the To Win series of books by Carroll Smith, which not only provides excellent technical explanations of the various aspects of race car setup and performance, but also driving advice. There is a long list of race driving texts which also serve to instruct how to improve your racing skills.

The best approach to improving real life race driving skills would be to enroll in a driving school and thus have skilled teachers pointing out proper technique and offering critique on your driving skills. Moreover, they provide a chance for actual time behind the wheel of a high performance road car and/or race cars on a race track, which is invaluable for learning driving skills quickly. In addition, taking part in local race events such as Autocross (also known as Auto-X, or Solo II) can be a low cost approach to learning real life car control using your own car.

Provide your own support

If you have learned some methods of improving your driving skills, it is advisable to help grow the sim community by offering help to those who could benefit from some of your experience. Aside from obvious forms of assistance (answering questions on forums or chat), you could also write a blog on a website devoted to sim racing, or if you have specific computer skills, you might be able to create or assist in the creation of websites or utilities which are useful to the sim community.

Otherwise, the best form of assistance you can give is by repaying others who have helped you develop your skills or taught you things you needed to know about sim-racing. Some helpful websites sometimes include a 'donate' button to provide you with a way to show your appreciation. Many such sites not only take the time and effort of the authors to construct and maintain the site, but also take some money to pay for the servers and domain name. Even a few dollars goes a long way in keeping these sites alive, and helping the sim-racing community.

Similarly, if someone provides setups that you routinely download and use to good effect, or if people provide excellent advice and support like creating a useful utility, think about offering a small iRacing gift certificate to reward them. It would allow them to buy more cars and tracks and encourage them to provide even more support in the future.

Driving Hints

Most of the hints I detail below are based largely on what I have learned through experience in driving and racing online at iRacing and to a lesser extent GPL many years ago. Most will be obvious to experienced racers, and many would be found in race driving texts. However, they are tips that I had found useful in progressing beyond a novice level, and hopefully they will help you to progress quickly.

Drive It Like You Borrowed It

Also known as 'drive it like you own it', though I like the 'borrowed it' version better, since it provides an extra incentive to bring the racecar back in one piece. I still struggle with this one myself, and often during practice sessions, I rack up far too many incident points. I am trying to resolve to keep the car under control at all times, as one would driving a real car on a track, since wrecking it against a wall would be an unthinkable expense. In iRacing you need only reset in most practice sessions, and rookie level races, but this encourages reckless risk-taking in car control and should be avoided as much as possible.

If you think of a car belonging to someone else, you will be sure to keep it on the track and not put it into danger of getting damaged.

This advice is well known in the racing community, and it remains one of the key points to keep in mind when starting out.

Be Precise

"What the ancients called a clever fighter is one who not only wins, but excels in winning with ease. ... He wins his battles by making no mistakes. Making no mistakes is what establishes the certainty of victory, for it means conquering an enemy that is already defeated."

-Sun Tzu

A driver who races with precision – who is always hitting their braking points and being consistent from lap to lap – will almost certainly outperform a driver who is generally faster, but less consistent. When a driver is pushing their limits and willing to accept a certain level of error, the price to be paid in time lost to spins and resetting the car will vastly outweigh the gains made by being a second or two faster on a successful lap.

Therefore one must always strive for control first to achieve consistency. Once that is accomplished it is easier to experiment with different lines, or carrying more speed through the turn, etc. in order to whittle your average time down in a controlled manner. Such a pattern of consistency will go a long way in achieving good race results early in your career, compared to most drivers who strive for speed first but lose so much time to errors.

Do not underestimate the effect that your simracing hardware (wheel and pedals) can have in this respect. In my experience, switching from a traditional potentiometer brake to a load-cell brake provided a big gain in consistency and having fewer incidents.

Minimize Input Lag

Experiment with ways to minimize input lag (the time it takes for your physical inputs to be shown in the display; one way of checking it is to snap the wheel from side to side as quickly as you can and watch for any delay in the display of the cockpit wheel, assuming you have it displayed). Input lag will make your responses slow and thus will compound any driving difficulties. Turning off V-Sync in the graphics options screen is one way to bring input lag way down (it can never be completely eliminated), but other graphics or sim settings may play a role. Some users found running V-Sync was fine as long as anti-aliasing (AA) and anisotropic filtering (AF) were configured in the video-card setup program ('CCC' for ATI cards) and turned off inside iRacing. Since every computer setup, hardware and drivers are different, it will be important to experiment with finding your own ways to limit input lag.

Contact patch comfort zone

Carroll Smith documents the different zones of comfort level for novice vs. experienced race drivers in terms of the amount of grip available from the contact patch of the tires. The experienced ones remain near the extreme edge of tire performance most of the time, while the novice either does not push hard enough or pushes too hard on the tire performance, resulting in a sudden loss of control.

To me this was enlightening since I began to think about staying on the safe side of tire grip, until I learned the braking points, gear selection, and proper line for each new track. Over time, you can begin to get comfortable and begin to push a little harder, without risking a loss of control.

Learn to feel the grip (FFB)

One of the best ways to feel the amount of available grip and whether you are pushing too hard is to use a force feedback wheel. I started iRacing using a non-FFB and after a few months I upgraded to an FFB wheel (Logitech Driving Force GT), and though it was a difficult adjustment to make at first, I began to see the value of being able to feel the level of grip the tires were providing.

I use a low level of force in my wheel so I am not really fighting against the forces, but still able to feel them effectively. Increasing the caster angle in the setup will provide more centering force in FFB wheels, but it may also make it more difficult to feel the loss of grip (so-called "pneumatic trail") when you exceed the optimum slip angle of the front tires.

Skidpad (Centripetal Circuit or any short track)

Driving schools often use skidpads to demonstrate the cornering limits of the tires and the car setup. A skidpad track is now available on iRacing but alternatively you could either use a wide expanse of asphalt or use a short track, such as South Boston. Before the skidpad track was available I began an experiment by taking a default setup on the Spec Racer Ford to the South Boston track in a test session and spent many laps getting a feel for how the car behaved in the turns and how my driving style affected my resulting speed coming out of the turns and down the short straight. Using the HUD split times and delta functions, I was able to improve my feel for the car and how it behaves around tight to medium radius turns, and the proper level of steering input to be fast and maintain control. I even ended up running the track in the reverse direction (obviously timing was impossible in this case), to be able to learn the same feel for right hand turns as well.

Putting in some time on the skidpad can teach you a lot about feeling the limits of the tires and how to maintain control while pushing as close to the limit as possible.

Concrete patches

Proper line around the track is essential to fast lap times. I found after a long time that keeping the outside wheels on the patches of cement at certain turns provide enhanced levels of grip, and allows you to carry much greater speeds through those turns.

Only certain turns on certain tracks have paved patches, but they are invariably in the spots which have the highest tire loading (the outside wheels), so it makes sense, first of all, that those are the locations where your outside wheels are supposed to be. Whatever the reason, there does seem to be a higher amount of grip on those patches which enables faster speed through the turns or getting on the throttle a little earlier than would normally be possible.

Fast pedals vs slow pedals

Many novice drivers struggle with oversteer more often than understeer, and the key reason for this is likely due to the more aggressive use of the pedals. The book 'Going Faster' discusses proper pedal technique in detail and mentions that faster application and release of the brake and throttle induces oversteer, while slower induces understeer.

Clearly, at least in my novice stage, I was applying and releasing throttle and brakes too fast to maintain control consistently. Once I read about this phenomenon, I was more conscious of this and began to maintain better control and encountered fewer oversteer problems than before. This has helped make me both faster and safer.

Countersteer when you must

A subset of the previous hint about pedal induced oversteer, are those cases where a fast transition is difficult to avoid. If I find a certain turn requires a fast mashing of the gas pedal, I now instinctively know that I should expect a little oversteer, and thus apply a small amount of countersteer (meaning simply not turning as sharply into the turn) momentarily. With practice, there is no loss of speed from wheelspin, and the amount of input on the steering wheel is barely noticeable. However, the result is better car control and faster acceleration through the turn.

Curbs and bumps

Since iRacing's tracks are laser-scanned, every detail of the track can be felt with high precision. And the tightest line around many of the turns at most road courses involves driving over curbs or getting very close to them. Entry and exit curbs are almost always safe to drive over at high speed, though with cars accelerating through the exit of turns at the edge of the traction limit, it may upset the car and result in a sudden spin if you are not ready for the curb. In certain instances this may mean easing off on the steering input slightly, assuming there is enough room to stay on the track. If you are running out of room and are risking putting a wheel off the track then it is a safer bet to ease off on the throttle rather than risk a spin.

Depending on the height of the apex curbs and the rebound settings of your car setup, you can either use the curbs or avoid them. Apex curbing is often flat enough to drive over safely, although tracks like Summit Point involve a few high curbs at apexes which must be avoided. Only experience gained through practice can show you which curbs need to be approached with extra care.

At Laguna Seca, all apex curbs can and should be driven over to optimize the lap. However, the red apex marking constitutes a severe bump at the inside of the curb, and if you take a too-tight line through the curb and run over the marking you will spin or have to slow down to almost a stop to collect the car.

Bumps in the road may not be apparent to the naked eye, but can be felt, particularly with force feedback wheels. If you understand the location of the dip or bump, you can learn to avoid it. In most cases, avoiding the bump or dip will allow for better control and speed. If your line accidentally leads you to a known bump you should prepare yourself by easing off on the pedal and steering inputs in order to not exceed the grip limits of the tires.

But in a few cases, slowing down too abruptly can itself be a hazard. At the last turn at Lime Rock Park, for instance, if you apply too much brake in the Skip Barber F2000 car you can actually bottom out the front of the car and induce a spin as the suspension compresses into the dip.

Lead With Your Eyes

As a rookie, there will undoubtedly be some 'uh-oh' moments where you're in a decision point about whether to keep you current pace and line or to back off and re-adjust to avoid trouble. When I was just learning sim-racing my instinct in these moments was to watch for the edge of the track and judge whether I was going to make it or not, and more often than not I was in for a rough ride.

In some cases it is a much quicker, thread-the-needle situation where you have to place the car perfectly or face the painful consequences. The best example of this was the chicane at Monaco in the Grand Prix Legends sim. If you missed your entry to the chicane by a few inches, your race was over, and I had many occasions to bury my car in the hay bales at that turn until I realized something critical. I was watching the hay bales while doing my best to avoid them. When I looked further up the track where I was aiming the car, I was able to safely make it through the chicane from that point onward, and what's more, at a much faster pace than before!

It seems obvious, but I think self-preservation instincts sometimes override logic and force us to look at the objects which threaten us. As a result, we take our attention off our target and thus set ourselves up for failure to hit the target.

By training yourself to keep your eyes always fixed on your intended path you can increase you success rate in making the turns as you intend and are able to make proper adjustments through the turns to ensure you hit your target reliably.

Adopt a home track

When I came out of sim retirement a few short months ago and got over some hardware upgrade issues to be able to run iRacing, I was struck with how much I had to learn. Since I had spent a few years with GPL 8-10 years ago, I thought I had enough car control experience with the 'Papy' model to be able to at least keep the car on the track for some slow laps until I got used to Laguna Seca and Lime Rock Park in the Solstice.

How naive. Perhaps I was just rusty, or the model had changed radically over the past 10 years, or the Solstice was just too different than any of the GPL cars I'd driven. Whatever the reason, it took a long while to get accustomed to the tracks and the level of grip.

The good thing about the rookie program is that it limits you to two tracks, so you don't easily get overwhelmed. Since I knew the layout of Laguna Seca from older sims, I grew accustomed to it much faster than Lime Rock as I knew the line and had a rough idea of the braking points. When the schedule flipped to Lime Rock Park I was immediately put off balance and felt unsure of myself, and relief would set in the following week when it would flip back to Laguna where - while slow - I could have a fighting chance of finishing the race without embarrassing myself.

After 'graduating' to a 4.0 safety rating and permitted to race the Skip Barber car, I was again a little overwhelmed with the new tracks I had to learn, along with the feel of the car which seemed more comfortable going down the track ass-first. Thousands of half-spins later I managed to teach my feet to go easier on the pedals, and that paid off with much more fun and less frustration.

But I still struggled to keep up with learning each new track that came up and spent most of the week learning not to spin, trying to be consistent, and finally getting brave enough for an end-of-week race. Late in my Rookie season, I decided to adopt a track.

We can all cite examples of world famous drivers, and local racing legends alike who are the driver to beat when the series lands at their home racetrack. A good example is former MotoGP champion, Nicky Hayden, who raced motorcycle events all across the US until making it up to MotoGP. When that series finally set up a race at Laguna Seca, he was automatically cited as the rider to beat, although he had struggled everywhere else until then. Sure enough, he ended up being the fastest guy there all weekend and walked away with the victory. The main reason was obviously that he had that track burned into his brain from all the racing he'd done there previously, and so when the other riders showed up there without any track time there, he led the way.

The trouble is, real life racers only have a limited number of tracks to study to that detail because of circumstances and geography. Those of us in iRacing don't have those constraints and can select any track on the system as our base.

I think this is a good strategy. Find a good track from your chosen series that has many different elements to learn from, and study it to death. I spent hours and hours at my chosen track (Lowes Road Course) until I had a good feel for it and could be competitive with people who were more advanced than me. I had practiced it to death in the Skip, since that was the car I raced at that track. But when week 13 came around they raced Solstices at Lowes RC, which was a blessing and a curse. A blessing since I'd studied that track to the minutest detail, and a curse, because I knew it so well in the Skip but not at all in the Solstice.

However, I practiced and quickly learned how to adjust for the different handling of the car and sure enough I held on for a victory in a Week 13 race when the leaders crashed out. A bitter-sweet victory, but my first as an online sim-racer! To celebrate, I immediately entered the next race, and the confidence boost helped me to attempt a couple of passes and I actually won again. This time, no fluke - and two in a row! I knew that it was an anomaly, and was not going to be a sign of things to come, but it showed the advantage of knowing the track well.

My skills have improved a lot over the past few months, and while I am still way slower than the aliens, and still fly off the track too much, I am improving on a daily basis. And I still see myself as one of the contenders when the schedule lands back at Lowes RC. I think that confidence boost when you land at your home track carries over to the next track as well. It may also be an advantage to race your home track earlier in the week when other drivers are still learning the track and thus you can exploit your advantage.

Moreover, you can retire early for the week and get a head start learning the next track with some offline practice, which can again keep you competitive the following week and allow you to punch above your weight. As time goes on you can select a new home track and use that training to apply to another series, knowing that if you return to your first home your brain will be ready for each upcoming turn.

As for what track to select, it will be different for everyone, but I would recommend a place that is not a popular or over-used track (e.g. Laguna Seca and Lime Rock Park, as they are raced all the time in the Rookie series) since most other drivers will know those tracks well. I would also find a track that includes elements you would expect to find at many tracks (heaving braking turns, high-speed turns, twisty sections, off-camber turns, etc.) so that the time spent studying your home track can be applied to similar turns at other tracks.

'Walk' the track

When learning a new track, a good technique that many real life drivers use is to walk or bicycle the racetrack the day before to study all the bumps, seams, curbing, dips, etc. so that they have an intimate understanding of all the track's features and foibles which can lead to an advantage over your competitors.

Obviously, in a virtual environment this is impossible, but a decent substitute is to do an offline session at the track and drive around the left side and then the right side at very low speed (~10 mph), as one would do by touring around on a bicycle. A third pass can be done to get a feel for the curbing on entry, apex and exit. This can help you understand which curbs can be attacked and which ones must be avoided or ridden on with care.

This simple process would only take 15-20 minutes (you can go faster down the straights), but may save you lots of time in getting up to speed and knowing where the bumps and dips are and how to adjust you line around the course accordingly.

Relax

When driving your sim racecar as fast as possible it is necessary to remain as relaxed as possible, even when the pace or action is pushing you to your limit. As your muscles tense up and your mind gets frantic, you begin to miss your marks and make bad judgments. Before an important session, allow a second to take a deep breath and flex your neck, arm and leg muscles to try to loosen up, and repeat this when possible during the event itself to maintain good driving reflexes.

Keep notes

Having a notepad or other way to quickly record your thoughts is important for several reasons. First, it can help you keep track of your setup changes and guide you through any necessary changes either to the setup or your approach to the corners. Having a track map is particularly useful in annotating with your thoughts about how the car handles and special notes about techniques or approaches to handling specific elements of the track. For this reason, sample maps are included in the Tracks section. Records of this nature may be important when you return to the track at a later date, and help you to prepare and get quickly up to speed.

In real racing, chances are you'll have people to help with running the car and getting things set-up to your liking - a race engineer/mechanic. In iRacing, you are the driver AND race engineer, so it makes sense to keep copious notes to refer back to when you need to make adjustments.

Another use for a notepad is writing down some impressions of your various competitors you are racing against, so that if you face them again, it may help you remember previous battles with them and what tactics may work and which ones do not. With so many racers on iRacing, having any kind of documentation at all would be helpful rather than only relying on your memory.

Finally, it is useful when someone provides advice during chat sessions so you can jot down some details for later use.

Setups

One of the most challenging aspects of iRacing is optimizing the car setup for your specific driving style. However, I believe that many novice drivers over-emphasize the necessity of an ideal setup, while many of the top drivers may be a bit overly dismissive of setup importance.

For novice drivers, there is much more time to be gained by using default setups, and focusing on improving your driving technique. If you find you are spinning a lot, it is more likely that you are too aggressive on the pedals, rather than because of a non- optimized roll-bar or camber setting. Once you have attained a safe and consistent level of performance, you can begin to look at the setup and make changes which suit the car, track (specific turns), and your driving style.

For experienced drivers, who spend most of the time at the limit of tire grip, perfecting the setup is more critical as it will allow the contact patches to be optimized in order to get the car around the track as fast as possible.

When pursuing car setups for various car and track combinations you can choose one of four options:

Option 1 - default
Using default setups is a good starting point for novice racers, since they were developed with the help of racing professionals, and are meant to provide a relatively neutral car which can be ridden safely by most novice drivers. However, once you have a good baseline level of skill and can reliably get the car to do what you want to on the track it may be time to think about other setup options.

Option 2 - free: stable
Several people who are adept at setups offer so called stable setups that are suitable for advanced rookies who want to try to get a little more speed without fearing a difficult handling car. In some cases they offer advice on setup tweaks for drivers to adjust as they become more comfortable with the car and track.

Option 3 - free: alien
Many of the top drivers, affectionately known as 'aliens' for their 'out of this world' car control, provide setups for their fastest laps. In some cases they even provide different setups for qualifying versus race or practice. Many novice drivers may struggle with alien setups due to the particular driving style required when running laps closer to the edge of traction. But some small adjustments can be done to make them more manageable for the general driving population.

For instance, aliens will quite often push the brake bias much further to the rear than most drivers in order to optimize the braking efficiency. However, novice drivers who do not have as fine brake control may have a much greater tendency to lock the rear wheels which will throw the car into a spin. Thus some basic adjustments such as brake bias and tire pressures may help to make alien setups more drivable by most drivers.

Option 4 - Starting from scratch
Using notes about the car's behavior is especially helpful in tweaking setups to adjust to your needs. The best starting point is probably the default setups and then making adjustments when necessary to get the car to behave the way that will make you fast and stable.

Be aware of two things. First, do not try to equalize the tire temperatures across the tire, especially for road courses, since the camber will change the aspect of the tire contact throughout the lap, but where it is most important is through the turns. Thus the feel of the car through the turns is more important than the end of session tire temperatures.

Secondly, tweaking the car setup starting with perfecting the behavior on the most important turns first. So if there is a turn that leads to a long straight stretch, it will be critical to carry as much speed out of that turn as possible to carry that speed advantage all the way down the straight. So setups changes such as camber and roll- bar settings may need to be made sub-optimal so that although handling may suffer on other turns, it will allow for winning back any lost time by having a strong balance for the critical turn. Then work on the next most important turn, until the best compromise setup can be found.

Having good setup resources are important when, like me, you have little or no experience in setting up a racecar. Tune to Win by Carroll Smith is an excellent starting point, along with the setup resource at the iRacing site, not to mention help from other iRacers. A setup guide is also provided in the section on Cars.

Practice and Focus

As a beginner, almost all of your brain activity is devoted to thinking about the car and how it is reacting to your inputs and making adjustments to keep control while going as fast as you can. With more practice and experience, your brain will not need to work nearly as hard. Car control will be hard wired, becoming more instinct and reflex, leaving your conscious brain more room for thinking. The danger in this, particularly for long races with few chances for battles, is that your mind may begin to wander and suddenly you find yourself making costly mental errors. The ideal situation is to have your instinct working on driving the car and your conscious brain working hard at race strategy.

Racing

Read and Understand the Sporting Code

As with any racing series, you should be aware of all the rules and obligations before entering your car in a race.

A large number of misunderstandings and confusion that come about on the forums with regard to racing incidents, scoring, etc. can be resolved by referencing the Sporting Code. Although it seems long, it is a fast read, and covers a broad range of topics in a very clear fashion. More importantly, by signing up with iRacing, you agreed to comply with the Sporting Code, so it is in your best interests to know your responsibilities when racing online.

A copy of the Sporting Code is provided at the end of this book as a reference. The updated version available at members.iracing.com stands as the genuine rules for the service.

Set Your Goals

Set realistic goals for your sim racing progress over the course of a season and keep in mind your time availability may change and will affect the pace of your progress. Set your goals over longer periods of time, so that if you encounter an unlucky stretch of bad results, you can still focus on meeting your long term objectives.

For individual races, you can set more achievable goals like zero incidents, finishing on the same lap as the leaders, or ending up in the top half of the field. Another common target is to finish at or above your expected finishing position (denoted by your assigned car number).

Focus your Efforts

"If he strengthens his left, he will weaken his right. If he strengthens his right, he will weaken his left. If he sends reinforcements everywhere, he will everywhere be weak."

-Sun Tzu

It is also important not to dilute yourself by racing too many different cars during the week. Each will require its own amount of skills and time to learn, and if you spend time in too many cars, you will not be able to maximize your pace in all. More likely, you will be outpaced by others who are more focused.

Preparing

"By failing to prepare you are preparing to fail."

— Benjamin Franklin

Scheduling

Trying to map out your weekly schedule can be a challenge for many. There are times when work schedules, travel, and family obligations require you to plan which days are available to race. Keeping tabs of your availability through a computer application like MS Outlook, or just a small daily planner book can go a long way to keeping your racing schedule realistic and fulfilling. You can combine this with the Race Planner feature on the iRacing Dashboard web page.

My weekly sim racing plan consists of practice for the first 2- 3 days (less for tracks I am confident on), then TT and qualify, followed by a race late in the week. Occasionally I will do additional races into the weekend if my schedule allows. If I finish racing early in the week, I may do some off-line practice to prepare for the upcoming week.

Although there is something to be said for lots of laps behind the wheel practicing, make some gaps in your week to take some time away and watch a movie or read a book, since excessive time devoted to one activity can lead to burnout, particularly if you have trouble achieving success toward your goals.

Kids, family, pets, telephone, etc.

Picking your schedule can be tricky enough, but you will have to deal with unexpected interruptions that a sim racer will need to cope with that a real race driver will not. Specifically, children, pets, and visitors will probably not appreciate the need for 100% focus on your race, and will often require you to divert your attention at a minimum or as can often happen - forfeit your race. So if you plan to race, it is best to pick a time and location where family obligations can be handled by someone else, and where you can be sequestered peacefully for the duration of the event. And make sure you reward the person shouldering the load by reciprocation!

There are many funny stories on the sim forums of people dealing with sudden interruptions by pets, usually attacking their feet, or suddenly blocking the view of the monitor. It's not uncommon, but a closed door is about the only way to prevent an untimely visit from a family friend.

I do the vast majority of my races after everyone else in the house has gone to bed, so for the most part I am free of having to answer the telephone or doorbell, or deal with someone desperate for a snack or fighting over a toy.

Hardware Preparation

Going into a race without even a cursory check of your hardware is the equivalent of a real race team not bothering to spend any time looking over the car before a race. Things like wheel and pedal calibration have caught many of us out at the wrong time, and will surely cost you any chance of a satisfactory result.

An important issue to consider is the stability of your racing hardware. If the pedal base is prone to sliding around, you will not have proper control of the car, and will probably end up with some muscle and joint aches afterwards. The cockpit itself, or chair on wheels, should be stable as well to prevent any unwanted change in position or having things fall from an unstable system during an event. A firm and fixed wheel and pedal are important to good performance during a race. Similarly, be aware of loose and dangling wires or other objects which can interfere with your driving movements.

Aside from yourself and your computer, your network connection is the third key element to a successful online race. Broadband DSL and cable are the only reliable connections most sim racers use, since satellite provides unacceptable lag times, and dial-up does not provide the throughput required. However, even a stable broadband connection can fail for a variety of reasons. First, an unexpected power disruption can bring down the modem and router if they (as well as your computer itself) are not set-up with a UPS (uninterruptible power supply). Without a UPS in place, it may be worthwhile keeping abreast of any severe weather patterns which could disrupt your race.

Another network connection problem occurs when the throughput drops too low due to a poor connection to the server. This could happen anywhere between the computer and the server but is often due to heavy network usage by other computers on the same network hub. So if you plan to take part in an important race, take precautions to shut down any other computers or equipment (video game consoles) which share the internet connection. Other systems, even if shut down, may come to life to download software updates, which can suddenly make your racing connection unstable. Similarly, your racing computer must be set up to only look for updates manually, and not automatically.

One method of avoiding these network sharing problems on modern routers is to use QoS (Quality of Service) settings to maintain optimal throughput through your sim racing link, while putting all other network traffic onto a lower priority so that the best connection to the server is maintained. Special gaming routers are specially set up to employ this feature in the best way.

Mind and Body

Your best performance is possible only when your mind is focused on the race. As such I recommend having your mind and body ready to take on a tough racing challenge.

Two important considerations are lack of sleep and alcohol consumption, both of which have a similar effect on your racing abilities in terms of judging distances and slow reaction times, which are both critical for racing. It goes without saying that a real racer would not put themselves on the grid after finishing off a couple of beers, so the same would have to be said if you want to avoid trouble on the virtual track. Of course, certain medications will also cause drowsiness. Being alert is the best way to fight a strong competitor. If you can't be alert, either take a night off and relax, or stick to offline sessions. Similarly, caffeine and other stimulants should be avoided before racing if they affect your ability to relax and make appropriate movements in a controlled way.

Also, it is important to do a bathroom break a few minutes before the start of a race, for obvious reasons. As well, a long race can make you quite thirsty, particularly when you can get overheated from the weather and intense racing battles, so having a refreshing beverage standing by is also important.

Practice Offline (Testing)

When learning a car and track combination for the first time, I recommend offline practice (you still need to be online, but you run the track alone), just to give you a clear track to focus on without any distractions. There is something to be said for having other drivers there to help you with advice, but I believe your first experience with a track should be done by yourself to learn the braking points and preferred line. Using split-time applications (iSpeed) is very useful in this stage to reinforce the things which are quick and to provide fast feedback on things which cost you time.

Having a clean track offline also helps when I am tweaking setups. This enables me to do a few installation laps at moderate pace to warm up the tires and then concentrate on how the car behaves around each turn without worrying about other cars trying to pass or forcing me to take a different line. In addition, if you are making changes to hardware settings or calibrations, it is best to do this in an offline environment for similar reasons.

Practicing online is an ideal place to get comfortable in battling with other drivers and learning how to pass without serious consequences. I also do special practice sessions offline which prepare me for overtaking. I do this by running a few laps as fast as I can on the right half of the track (no cheating at apexes), and then similarly on the left half of the track. The goal is to learn how to keep control of the car and change your braking points when you have to go to the inside or outside to complete a pass. If you only practice the ideal line, you will quickly lose control if you do not adjust your braking points and control expectations when you are sharing the turn with another car beside you.

Practice Online

"If you know the enemy and know yourself you need not fear the results of a hundred battles. "   *- Sun Tzu*

There are thousands of people sim racing on iRacing, and more joining every day, so it is impossible to know the character of all the drivers you will be racing against. Some will be cautious rookies, some will be aggressive and others reckless, some will be trustworthy, and you will need to keep your distance from others. Some will be much faster, and others may be much slower than you.

There are several ways to get to know your competition before the start of a race. First, by racing the same series at similar days and times, you will begin to recognize names and their associated skills and behavior. But mainly, entering practice sessions for your favorite series will expose you to the main competition you will face. During these sessions, keep track of who the fast drivers are, who maintains a pace like your own, and who are the slower drivers. When racing these names at a later point, you will recognize who may be attacking you and you can choose whether to fight aggressively or concede.

As well, watch other drivers for their chosen line, whether they are late brakers, or if they struggle with a certain part of the track. That way, if you encounter them in a race shortly thereafter you will know which areas they may be more vulnerable to a pass.

Time Trial (TT) - find your 'safe pace'

Once you have sufficient amount of practice on the track, and are comfortable in keeping a consistent pace without losing control (if you are losing control, you are pushing the car beyond your abilities, and need to slow down), then it is time to do a time trial. This is a good tool for teaching you discipline about maintaining a safe and consistent pace. I find that the first couple of laps I am quite slow, since the tires are cold and I need to get into a rhythm.

As the session progresses, I find confidence in the grip of the car and can begin to be a little more aggressive on the throttle accelerating out of turns, so my pace usually improves. If you go too fast there is a big price to pay if you lose control: first you will risk suffering a safety rating penalty, plus, you must start your consecutive lap counter over. If the incident is severe enough to damage the car, you will probably have to reset and warm up the tires again for a few laps. Thus, this is a good session to learn how to drive within safe limits, while maximizing your pace.

Qualify

Qualifying for your race is highly recommended since it gives you a clear advantage of starting ahead of the people that choose not to qualify.

The downside is that, unless you are fast enough to be at the front, you will be surrounded by cars as you accelerate into the first turn, which - especially in the rookie series - can be a dangerous place to be. With care and practice you can learn to avoid this trouble. Opting out of qualifying or starting from pit-lane (by waiting until everyone takes the start before pressing the green 'race' button), can still yield a good result or even a win, but you have to rely on poor driving or bad luck for those in front of you, and care and skill on your part.

That is why, even with the increased risk of damage in the first couple of turns, the benefits of qualifying and getting a few spots ahead will pay off in the long run. As well, a few bad experiences, though painful, will teach you something about how to learn to spot trouble before it happens.

Qualifying itself is much like a TT session, with a greater emphasis on your safety rating. So putting in many clean laps can help to pull up your safety rating faster than a TT session, and it will not adversely affect your TT rating. Take the first few laps with great caution until you can feel the extra grip from the tires, and then slowly work on hitting your marks and keeping consistent until you can bring your times down with an acceptable margin of error. If other drivers are present use the F3 information display to be aware of other drivers so you do not interfere with someone's fast lap unintentionally.

Preparing to Race

After deciding you are ready to race, and have enough practice to know your lines and braking points, and how to drive off the ideal line when necessary, there are a few things to consider before the green light.

Examine the Grid

The first thing I do when landing in a race session is to check my grid placement. If you've practiced and qualified enough with other drivers, you should have some expectation of where you should be gridded, but depending on the split you may end up happily surprised or disappointed. In most cases you will end up similarly placed as your online practice sessions indicate.

Look for familiar names from practice and qualifying sessions and try to recognize any drivers ahead of you who you think may be slower than you on average, or conversely, faster drivers who may be behind you, as these are the drivers you may have to deal with during the race.

Examine the Entry List

Next step is to go to the 'Entries' tab to look over the list of drivers and see whose connection may be problematic. If someone has high ping times or low connection quality, you have to take note of these drivers, and keep a safe distance from them, as the server may think your cars are hitting each other even though on your end you look to be safe, and thus get unexpected incident points. Take special care to not brake late when following them and to give extra room when trying to pass, particularly if their car appears to be blinking from poor connection quality. If they warp (fast repositioning on the track when the computer prediction of the car's location is suddenly corrected with fresh data), you may suddenly find the car you thought was beside or behind you is now on top of you.

So take extra time to study the names of drivers who require an extra margin of space to avoid any netcode surprises.

Warm-up

The next step is to do at least one warm-up lap. Some drivers do not bother with this, since there is a risk of damage which counts against your safety rating, but I find that one lap will help get your mind ready for each turn with the same grip level that you will have on cold tires at the start. So it is like a practice start. There is no need for bravado or trying to set the fastest warm-up time, as there is no benefit for doing so.

Moreover, there may be some advantage to having the competition think you're slower than you really are.

After finishing your warm-up lap, you can exit and watch the driving habits of those who you think you will be fighting for position with. Observe their lines, braking points, car control skills, speed, and passing ability to look for any weakness that you can use to your advantage during the race.

Last minute checks

When awaiting the start of the race (after the warm-up), take a second to review your setup to ensure it is correct for the race session, and also that you have a sufficient quantity of fuel. If unsure, ask the other drivers, and in most cases they will let you know.

When you grid your car, take a second to scroll to the pit refueling information screen (default = F5 key), and uncheck the refuel check box. That way if you have the option to reset the car after an incident, you won't have to wait an extra 10 seconds in the pits while they add unneeded fuel to your car.

Consider T1 and T2 strategy

As you await the green light, take a second to think about what your strategy will be as you enter the first two turns. Try to be as conservative as possible as most accidents in races will occur in the first few turns. It is not a rookie problem - most Formula 1 races will have accidents in the first few corners. But be prepared and leave enough of a gap in front to allow for reaction time if the person ahead brakes earlier than you expect. Have an escape plan in mind if you have to dodge cars and know how the curbing may affect those decisions.

The Race

If you're like me the flash of the green light is matched with a surge of adrenaline, but the key thing is to remain calm and make rational choices and keep within your safe pace to keep the car on the track.

The Start

The start is the most dangerous part of the whole race as the cars are close together and all fighting for as many positions as possible. Taking care to know how to handle the car and situational awareness of where other cars are and will be is paramount to getting through safely.

On grid: set your take-off RPM

For road course standing starts, it is important to know how fast to rev the engine as you wait to select 1st gear. Note that since clutch and transmission damage is not yet modeled you can simply select 1st gear with high revs without fear of damage or stalling.

But in practice sessions you should practice taking off from a standing start and learn what rpms will provide the fastest getaway. For instance the Skip Barber F2000 car can rev at the limit without fear of wheelspin, while the Spec Racer Ford should be around 4500 rpm before dropping into 1st gear to get the best launch.

Do not guess on the lights - be sure.

Sometimes you will get impatient waiting for the green light and try to anticipate the green to get a good start. Never attempt that, since any slight movement will result in a black flag which forces you to make a costly pit stop or face disqualification.

Another common mistake is to set off when the lights appear on screen for a few seconds and then turn red. It is not unusual to see drivers lurch forward when that happens, and then have to deal with a black flag penalty. Be aware that the lights will go from off to red before turning green, so it may be worth reminding yourself of that sequence as you sit on the grid.

Know your braking point for T1 - be safe!

Approaching T1 is often where the aggressive drivers hope to gain the most spots, and often they will be the guys who end up in the grass, watching the field stream by.

If you are starting at the front, be aware that cold tires will not have a high level of grip and thus you will need to brake a little earlier and less aggressively for T1 at the start. It will take practice to strike a compromise of safety and protecting your position with quickness. But always choose a safe T1 over a fast one, since the risks are not worth it.

If you are starting in the middle of the grid you need even more care since you not only also have to deal with cold tires, but also the many other drivers fighting for position on similarly cold tires. Respect and care need to be in vast supply to get everyone through safely. Even losing a couple of positions is a satisfying result if you make it through unscathed and can settle into your pace with a healthy car, ready for battle.

If you are at the back, the pressure is off and you can hang back a little and watch for accidents from a safe distance and be ready to pounce on others misfortune. It is not unusual for a driver starting at the back of the grid or from pit lane, to start conservatively and be in the middle of the pack by the end of lap 1.

Attacking

Once you settle into a position after the first few turns it is time to employ your racing strategy. Know what drivers you can attempt to pass, and think about where their weak points or your strong points may present a passing opportunity.

Have a look occasionally

When attacking a driver ahead of you who is similar to your pace or slower, follow them for a few turns to learn their driving style and braking points. Occasionally, if I get too close I will pull my car to the inside as a conservative move so that I do not run into the back of the car ahead when entering the next turn. Occasionally when I do this the driver will slow down and allow me past, much to my surprise and delight. They are just trying to be conservative and safe, and although that was my intention as well, they've given me the bonus of a free pass.

Not all passes are that easy, but when you are given the opportunity, seize it.

Try to disrupt their rhythm

In one recent race I was slightly faster than the driver ahead of me but he was skilled and competitive and never allowed me a good opportunity to safely get by. His braking points were similar to mine and I could not take advantage enough to make a full pass. After several laps of increasing despair, I decided to try to throw off his rhythm by braking abnormally early for a turn which he normally braked quite late for.

I believe he noticed my abnormally premature braking and this must a have triggered a question in his head such as "why did he brake there ... or am I braking too late all of a sudden" and sure enough he locked up his brakes, started to lose traction on entry and spun the car around. After 4-5 laps of following him closely and keeping a predictable pace, I was able to disturb his rhythm enough to provide a passing opportunity, for even if he didn't spin out, his poor turn entry would have provided a way for me to attack on the next straight.

Choose your moment
Obviously if you are much faster than the driver ahead of you, you will need to get by as soon as you can find a safe way to do so. Here again, by knowing the driver's style, speed, line, braking points, and weaknesses, you can plan where to attack. If you follow too closely, you may not only risk a collision, but also may not leave enough room to build your momentum to speed past them down the straight. So leave a little extra room on turn entry if your plan is to follow them through the turn and pass them on the next straight.

Clearly, if the plan is to pass them under braking for a turn then you must follow as closely as possible down the straight to draft behind them and then pull out well before you know they will start to brake. Be sure to brake early enough if you are not on the ideal line, so you don't run into their side going through the turn.

Here is where practicing unconventional lines around the track can pay dividends.

Defending
It can be very unnerving to be followed by someone closely who you have to trust will not ram you off the road accidentally. They will sometimes wait patiently behind you for any slight mistake which allows them an opportunity to get by. The key thing in this case is to focus most of your attention on your driving and being as clean and consistent as possible. You need to be aware if they attempt a pass, but you should not let them distract you from your primary task of driving your own car as quickly and safely as possible.

Slow in, fast out
In general, my improvement in lap times has come about from realizing that I was braking too deep into the corners and frantically trying to get the car to turn in, and ending up losing a lot of speed through the apex as a result. So I began to back up my braking to father away from the turn so I could turn the car in easily and get back on the power sooner. The big advantage is that I have a lot faster exit speed which gains a lot of time by the time you finish the next straight stretch.

There lots of more talented drivers who can brake much later than I - nearer the edge of the traction limit - and get back on the throttle early. Others also brake later but have trouble launching off the corner in the same way I struggled in the past. I have an edge over these drivers when defending my position because, although they may close on me going into the turn, my better getaway from that turn pulls me out of reach down the next straight. This dance continues for as long as I can stay consistent. If I keep it up, the driver may get frustrated and start making mistakes, which will allow me to maintain my position.

A defensive line

When under attack from another driver who is trying to draft it is important not to weave your car around, which is a protestable practice. Chose one line and stick to it, but chose carefully as you will have to live with the consequences. If the track is wide enough consider a central path down the straight, as it will open up two tricky passing lanes for the attacker - neither of which is ideal. If they choose the outside lane, they may be able to brake slightly later, but will have an inferior line going into the turn apex if you are able to maintain the preferred line. It will also force them to take care not to touch the grass in the braking zone as they squeeze by, and may cause them to slow down for caution's sake.

If they chose the far inside lane, they will have to brake earlier and will have to deal with a sharp entry line, which will take away much of their momentum.

Only perform this defense if you trust the driver behind, because the margin for error is low and you will both need to be aggressive and careful simultaneously.

In lieu of this line, you will have to choose the inside or outside lane, and both offer advantages and disadvantages. There is no one correct choice and the better path will vary depending on the section of the track, the aggressiveness of each driver, the car control and confidence of each driver, and a thousand other factors. Online practice is the best way to become familiar with defensive tactics.

Conceding

If someone behind is much faster than you, think about whether conceding the position may be a better strategy than risking an accident.

For example, in one race a Summit Point - Jefferson, I ended up with a faster driver behind me after we both had separate lap 1 incidents. I knew the driver was aggressive after watching his warm-up and lap 1 off track excursions, so I let him by without a fight and followed him from a safe distance. He managed to intimidate several drivers into running off the track as a result of following dangerously close, and knocked a few more off when tussling for position. Nothing was illegal or protest-worthy in his driving, but he was by far the most aggressive driver I had seen in a while. In every case, I was able to follow him past all the other unfortunate drivers who tried to fight for position rather than opting for a safer concession. I would probably have not been able to safely pass several of those drivers, but the door was opened for me. Before long his race ended prematurely (another accident) and I inherited his second position, after being at the tail of the field not far from the start, and managed to finish second in the race. It is one clear example where letting a faster driver through can pay dividends, and where fighting too hard to keep your position from a faster driver can be costly.

The best place to concede a position or to be lapped is to wait for a straight stretch and pull to the side which is not the ideal line, and when your intentions are clear to the following driver, back off the throttle a little to allow them by cleanly. Try not to bleed off all your momentum, or you could end up losing positions you hadn't intended to. Allowing a car to pass on a turn is a more risky choice, and can sometimes lead to misunderstandings and accidents. Keep your line through the turns and concede on the straights is the best strategy I have found.

Lapped traffic

Accidents are inevitable, and one of the most frustrating is between leaders and lapped traffic, and the fault is usually shared between both drivers to some degree.

First, be aware of other drivers near you on the track. Use the F3 information box to know who you are battling for position with (their names are in white), who is traffic you have lapped or are about to lap (names are in blue), and people who are a lap ahead of you or are about to lap you (names in red).

When the names in red start to get within a few seconds of your position, then you may see a blue flag being displayed in the top corner. This is to let you know that there is a car approaching who is close to lapping you. The blue flag is for information only and does not obligate the driver to suddenly slow down - this is a recipe for disaster!

If you are genuinely as fast or faster than that car you can disregard the blue flag, so long as your car doesn't impede the pace of the lapping car. However, in most cases they have gotten to that position by being faster than you and you should begin to look for a safe place to concede the position. As mentioned in the previous section, look for a straight stretch to allow the driver past and avoid mid-corner concessions. There is no firm obligation for the lapped car to slow down or concede the place, but neither should they aggressively fight for position, particularly if the position has already been conceded. Re-passing the leader to get onto the lead lap should only be done if the leader is prepared for the pass, and you can sustain a faster pace once past (so as not to slow their pace).

If you are trying to pass a lapped car, you have to understand that it is not obligatory for them to easily concede the spot, and moreover they are expected to hold their racing line through the turns. As such, you need to think about where is the safest spot to pass (usually down a straight), and make clear and decisive movements so that your intentions are not misunderstood. Once you get alongside a lapped car they should have common sense enough to concede the position gracefully and safely so that neither driver loses much pace on the rest of the competition.

Invariably, misunderstandings complicated by netcode issues will lead to accidents with lapped traffic. If you are following a leader who is about to lap a slower driver be ready to pounce on any mistake. Similarly, if you are battling with a driver and both of you are about to be lapped, be smart about how you concede the position. For instance, if you allow the leader through on a straight without losing much time or momentum, and the driver you are battling with then allows the leader through in a more clumsy way, it could allow you to follow the leader past the driver and thus gain an easy position.

Consult the Sporting Code for advice on lapped traffic and what is expected of each party.

Recovery from an accident

Inevitably, you will have accidents with other cars or by yourself during a race. In those situations it is important not to lose excessive amounts of time getting back on the track and back on pace, all while doing so safely, of course.

If you find yourself in danger of going off course at the exit of a turn, ease off the throttle to see if the car will resume a safe exit line. If it still looks to be un-savable straighten your wheel and get off the pedals and see if the car can then be coaxed back on the track in a controlled fashion. Applying throttle with one side of the car on the grass needs to be done with extreme care to avoid spinning out.

Take care since the grass is known for its slipperiness, and if you are sliding off into the grass, try to minimize your inputs to regain control. If you are heading for a wall try pumping the brakes or feel the braking intensity through the FFB to try to minimize chances of damage against a wall or trackside object.

If you end up off track without hitting anything, your car will probably be undamaged and you simply need to re- establish yourself on the track. If you are off-track near the apex of a corner, it makes sense to only re-join the track if there are no cars approaching (use the F3 information box and your look-left/look-right functions). If there are cars nearby, ride the grass parallel to the track until you can re-join at a safer spot.

If you are on the racing line but spun out, and you know cars are approaching, you need to think whether moving off the track can be done safely and quickly. If your car is damaged then reset or escape as soon as possible to avoid other cars being collected in the accident. If your car is still drivable and if drivers have a way by you and you try to move off track you can risk more carnage. So if you are near the edge of the track it would make sense to move your car further off track as soon as you can. But if you've spun out in the middle of the track with cars approaching, hold your position and hope that smoke or yellow flags will put the drivers on notice about trouble ahead so they can plan to watch for you and find their way around you. Once the track is clear, then you can move out of the way and safely resume if your car is undamaged.

If you have contact with another car you need to assess if your car has sustained any damage which will affect its driving behavior. In open-wheeled cars, this can sometimes be seen by simply looking at the wheels to see if they are misaligned or otherwise out of place. If the car suddenly feels different (oversteer or understeer) or you have to hold the steering wheel at an angle to go straight, then it will probably need to be retired or reset (if it is available in your race).

If you choose to reset, the best strategy is to decide if you will lose more time completing the lap in a broken car, or if you should reset on the spot. If your car is fairly drivable and you can get close to a racing pace without risking damage to others, you can probably complete a half-lap to go near (but not past) your pit stall and then reset. Cars are towed forward around the racetrack, so in order to minimize towing time you should be as close to your pit stall as is reasonable. If you go past, or just cannot safely maneuver your car without endangering others, you'll have to cope with a longer tow back to the pits.

You needn't enter the pits, as that will require you to slow down further, wasting even more time. Just drive off-line to stay out of the way, and then reset. If you configured your pit-stop in advance, you will not have to wait for the car to be re-fueled and should then be able to proceed right away. Be aware that you will be on cold tires again so drive accordingly.

If you are more than half a lap away from your pit, and/or your car is severely damaged, the best option is to reset on the spot. In many cases, that can mean going a lap down on the leaders. That is a big penalty to pay for a small mistake, which is why you always need to drive with extra caution. Particularly on tracks without lots of run-off room, where a mistake is more likely to bend up the car.

Repair features are planned for future iRacing updates, which will change strategy. In any event, the cost in lost time and track position is never worth the risk of pushing the car beyond your skills.

Post-Race

When you cross the finish line you can choose to complete the lap, which is subject to incident penalties to the same degree as warm-up laps until the last car finishes (after that incidents no longer count against your safety rating). Most drivers choose to stop shortly after crossing the finish line. This is not a problem unless they block the track for other drivers following close behind, and thus risking a big accident. The best approach is to slowly pull off-line to the edge of the track and slow down in a controlled fashion so that drivers approaching from behind are not caught off guard. Once your speed is below 30 mph, you can pull off the track without penalty before stopping and exiting the track.

Drivers at the end of the race generally fall into one of two categories - those who are elated and exhilarated with the race and the others who are indifferent or frustrated/angry. Both groups tend to exit the session immediately, which takes away a chance to discuss the race and any incidents which could be reviewed for discussion. It also is an opportunity to form friendships and camaraderie within the community.

Another mistake made by happy and angry racers alike in their excited state is forgetting to save the replay after the race. Saving the replay is important since it allows you to critique yourself and judge what things you did right and what you did wrong. This is an important part of learning from your mistakes. Moreover, if there are other battles going on, you can learn a lot from how other drivers handle passing attempts, and reacting to the unexpected.

Debrief - what did you learn?

After leaving a session, you should take lots of notes on several aspects of the race:
- quality of the setup; note parts of the track where handling was a problem
- behavior of the competition
- special aspects to remember about the track
- things learned during battles
- self-critique your driving performance and your mental focus
- evaluate your race strategy, how it evolved during the race and if it was successful or not
- areas to improve

Taking notes is a critical step to improving but they are only useful if you act on the observations and learn from them. Keeping records and acting on them will help you learn faster and make fewer mistakes as you gain experience. Organizing your notes by track or series can help you refer back when you return to the track at a later date.

Another important learning tool is to load up the replay and use it to learn:
- what things you and others did during the race which worked well
- what things you and others did during the race which failed
- study battles all over the track with care and especially note successful passes and rewind further back to understand how the pass was set up and completed
- review the start of the race and analyze any incidents and who made it through successfully and observe how they did so
- use the cockpit view in most cases to see what others see, and supplement with Zeppelin or chase views to get perspective on car position
- resist the urge to pretend to drive the car with steering and pedal inputs, since the true link between your brain and the sim is not present, and may inadvertently instill some bad habits

Statistics

One aspect of sim racing many drivers enjoy is following their (and friends') progress with statistics. IRacing is well suited to handle this with endless statistics for each series, track, club, country, division, etc. in terms of lap times, points, incidents, iRating, safety rating, wins, laps led, etc. When you set goals for progress, statistics can be a good way to set a firm target and then gauge your progress and know whether you are achieving your goals.

But don't fall into the trap of unhealthy focus on iRating or safety rating. Obsessing over this will take away much of the fun of sim racing and will only amplify the frustration when things go wrong, and will thus be a downward spiral of aggravation. Race as fast and clean as you can and the results will come and your SR and iRating will settle into your own specific iRating level which will bounce around from result to result, but within a narrow range. Should your skills improve, you may see a gradual improvement, but do not concern yourself with sudden spikes, or even a string of bad results - it happens to everyone. When your iRating drops, you will end up in lower strength of field splits and/or a bigger iRating bonus for a given result so you'll end up finishing with increasing iRatings.

Protesting

Many new drivers will experience a bad race or series of races, as rookie series are full of inexperienced drivers, all anxious to finish well, and often beyond their driving limits.

When incidents or aggressive mishaps occur between drivers, tempers will flare. At times you will have to deal with furious chat (harsh language is protestable so don't do it - chats are recorded) immediately after the incident or after the race is finished - please keep voice and text chat during the race to an absolute minimum as it distracts other drivers. Also keep in mind that many drivers cannot write text messages while driving and may not have voice chat enabled, so as not be distracted while racing so cannot apologize. So if you don't receive an apology when you believe the other driver was responsible, do not presume you know what their intentions were.

Most drivers have no intentions of causing trouble for others. Most aggressive-looking moves are the result of the limitations of internet communications relaying positions of each driver as accurately as possible, rather than any poor driving decisions you observe on your end. Their replays may look completely different than yours. The longer the lag for each driver, the more different the computer perspectives will appear. In addition, in some cases, you will be quite distant from another car, but still be given incident points due to the different perspectives on each computer.

If you do not get to address the incident with the other driver during the race session, you can attempt to contact the driver by private message, which you can find by entering the iRacing forums page. There is no guarantee that the driver in question opens the forums and sees your private message. If you cannot get a response, you should file a protest at protest@iracing.com. Follow the guidance of Sporting Code when filing a protest. Having a replay will be important to back up your accusations, particularly if the other driver has a replay of his own.

The worst thing you could do is post a thread on the forums complaining about the incident or a string of similar incidents, since all others have had to deal with the same thing and do not enjoy reading rants. Keep in mind that naming the other driver in your rant and including a replay of the incident are very bad etiquette and may result in being protested yourself. Use the forums for constructive purposes and you will find it will encourage others to do the same.

The easiest way to sleep at night is to not get upset but submit the protest and move on with your driving. If the other driver was truly at fault and it was intentional or reckless, they will be punished. The FIRST sporting code and protest system is well respected and one of the true advantages of iRacing over other sim-racing options.

iRacing.com™ Car Specifications

iRacing has a breadth of content and a wide variety of cars available and under development. Having so much choice is wonderful, but can also be a little daunting for beginners. There is no reason to feel left out if you only race the lower powered cars, and indeed, many people who have been with the service since the beginning run primarily the lower powered cars.

Why? There are lots of reasons, but principle among them has to be the feel of the cars which is most acute in some of the rookie and D series cars. Also the limited number of setup options mean it is easy to jump into a car and learn how to drive without wondering if the faster folks have some magic setup at work. As well, since the cars have a greater number of drivers available (people of all license levels can drive them) there are plenty of populated races and practice sessions to enjoy at any given time, and the brevity of the events is attractive for people who cannot devote long hours preparing for and racing at the higher license level events which are typically much longer duration.

This section tries to capture a flavor for what each car is like and what makes it tick. It contains some information one would expect to find in an owner's manual or a car magazine review article. There's a lot of data for enthusiasts to pore over, but the key thing is just to understand some basics about the car and how it performs. Advanced users can make use of the power and torque curve to understand about optimum shift points and performance expectations. The Skip Barber and Spec Racer Ford cars have a range of setup options which are detailed for each car, along with the baseline setup values. Thus people working on their own setups can use these as a guide.

At the end of the car specifications section are a couple of plots to show how the cars compare to each other in terms of grip level and also the engine torque which is related to the bore and stroke ratio.

Note that I have gleaned most of the performance data from testing within the simulation, and much of the other information was obtained from public websites or iRacing.com. Some assumptions were made in some of the more complex calculations - so if any discrepancies exist, one should trust data published from manufacturers and teams with true data.

Finally, there are tables which guide users on how to tinker with the setups of the Spec Racer Ford and Skip Barber F2000 cars in order to cure any persistent handling problems, or to help tweak a setup to suit your style of driving.

Pontiac Solstice (Rookie Class)

One of the first elements to the service and frequently the first car for most rookie road racers on iRacing.com™, the Pontiac Solstice (often jeeringly referred to by less flattering names) is a good car for beginners. It has limited amounts of power and conventional rear wheel drive which is a good way for beginners to learn car control on the racetrack with a vehicle not drastically unlike their ordinary road car. It is very much a 'momentum' racecar since you need to keep up your speed through the turns as much as possible to be competitive, which is a challenge with the limited amount of grip from the tires.

The advanced rookie car has setup options, but the rookie version does not, and since the car used for the advanced rookie series was replaced with the Spec Racer Ford, efforts to work on setups for this car have ceased.

Still, even experienced iRacers enjoy spending time in the car and helping rookie driver acclimatize to the service during rookie events or practice servers.

General

Style	2 door convertible
Drivetrain	Front engine, rear wheel drive

Tires

Size	P245/35R18
Circumference	77.7" | *1.97 m*
Radius	12.3" | *0.312 m*
Construction	Radial (dry racing tire)
Tread	Slick
Wheel size	18 x 8"

Suspension, Steering & Brakes

Front suspension	Fully independent 'FE3'
Rear suspension	Fully independent 'FE3'
Steering	Power assisted, rack and pinion
Steering Ratio	16.40 : 1
Turns, Lock-to-lock	2.7
Brake type	discs front and rear; power assist brakes
Brake bias	Slight front bias
Braking aid	ABS

Engine

Specs	2.4L, 4 Cyl DOHC normally-aspirated Ecotec LE5 w/ var. valve timing
Compression Ratio	10.4 : 1
Horsepower	181 hp | *135 kW* @ 5800 rpm
Torque	231 lb-ft | *314 N-m* @ 4800 rpm
Weight : Power ratio	16.6 lb/hp | *10.1 kg/kW*
Power : Weight ratio	0.0603 hp/lb | *0.0992 kW/kg*

Drivetrain

Transmission	5 speed manual
Differential	Limited slip
Gear Ratios	
1st	3.75:1
2nd	2.26:1
3rd	1.51:1
4th	1.00:1
5th	0.73:1
Final Drive Ratio	3.91:1

Aero

CdA	7.87 ft^2 | *0.731 m^2*
Frontal Area	22.0 ft^2 | *2.04 m^2*
Drag coefficient, Cd	0.36

Dimensions

Weight in sim	3000 lb | *1361 kg*
Weight Distribution F/R	50% / 50%
Wheelbase	95.1" | *241.5 cm*
Track Width F/R	60.7" / 61.5" | *154.3 cm / 156.1 cm*
Height	50.9" | *129.3 cm*
Width	71.3" | *181.1 cm*
Length	157.2" | *399.3 cm*
Center of Gravity Height	20 " | *50.8 cm* (approx)

Performance

Top Speed	123 mph | *198 kph* (no draft)
Skidpad Lateral acceleration	
@50m | 165 ft	0.99 G (49.6 mph | *79.8 kph*)
@150m | 492 ft	0.98 G (85.1 mph | *137.0 kph*)
Max Forward Acceleration	0.54 G
0 - 100 kph (62 mph)	7.3 s
Optimal Shift RPM	
$1^{st} - 2^{nd}$	6900
$2^{nd} - 3^{rd}$	6900
$3^{rd} - 4^{th}$	6900
$4^{th} - 5^{th}$	6300
Braking 100 – 50 kph	1.35 s
Braking 100 – 0 kph	2.92 s (ABS) … 2.72 w/o lock-up
Max Deceleration	1.13 G

Cars iRacing Paddock Page 55

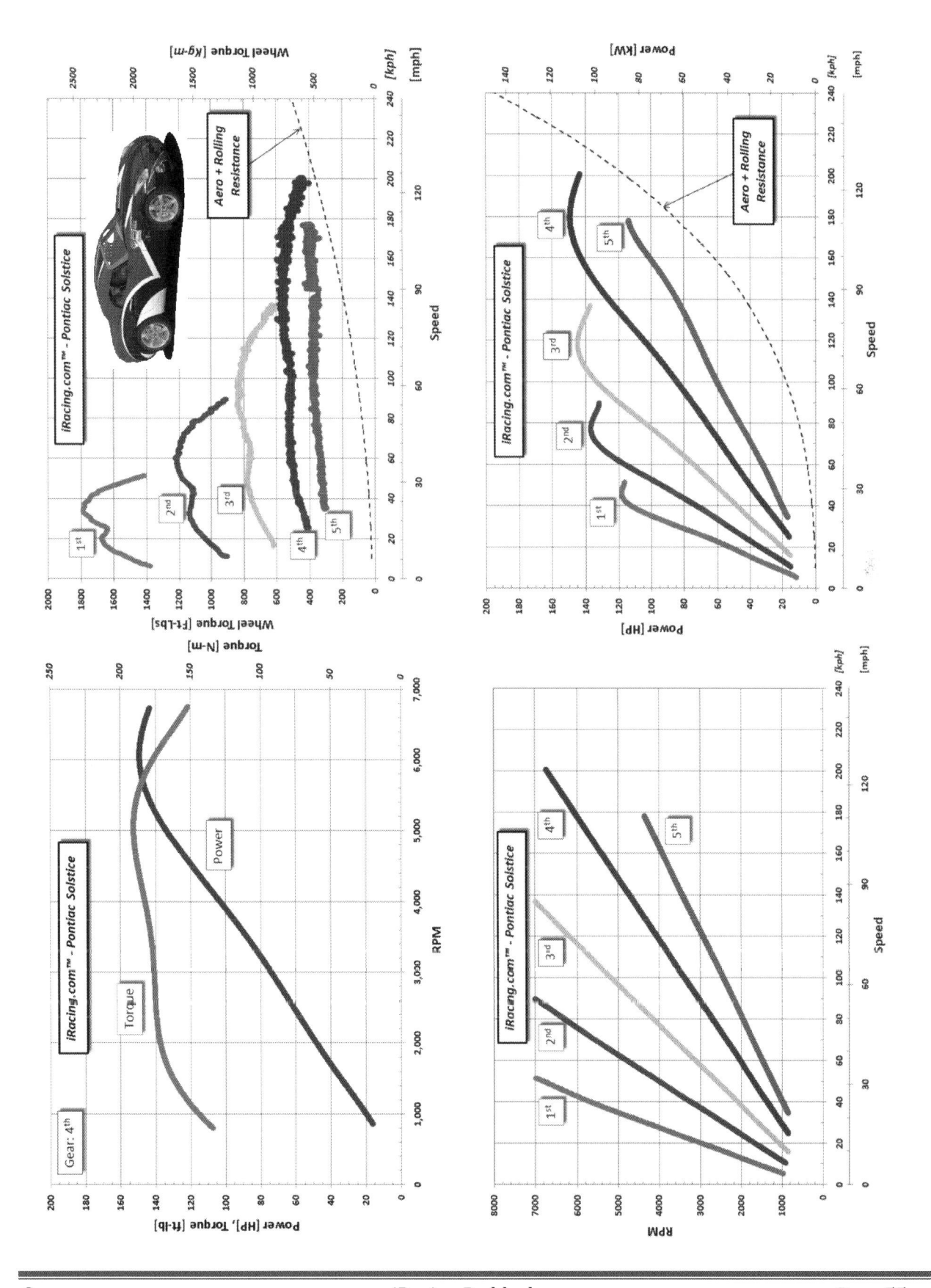

Baseline Setup for non-Rookie Solstice {range for each option}

No setup options are available for the Rookie Solstice car. The settings below apply to the non-Rookie car but the Rookie car maintains the baseline settings from the non-Rookie car. They are shown here for information purposes only.

Tire Pressures	
Front L/R	30.0/30.0 psi {16.0 – 40.1 psi} | *207/207 kPa {110 – 276 kPa}*
Rear L/R	30.0/30.0 psi {16.0 – 40.1 psi} | *207/207 kPa {110 – 276 kPa}*
Toe In	
Front	-2/16" {-5/16" - $^+$5/16"} | *-3.2 mm {-7.9 - $^+$7.9 mm}*
Rear	$^+$2/16" {-5/16" - $^+$5/16"} \| *$^+$3.2 mm {-7.9 - $^+$7.9 mm}*
Camber	
Front L/R	-2.1° / -1.8° {-2.7° - $^+$0.3° / -2.3° - $^+$0.7°}
Rear L/R	-1.2° / -1.3° {-2.2° - $^+$0.8° / -1.8° - $^+$1.2°}
Caster	
Left Front	$^+$6.6° {$^+$5.1° - $^+$8.6°}
Right Front	$^+$6.7° {$^+$5.1° - $^+$8.6°}
Fuel	13.9 Gallons | *52.6 L {2.6 – 13.9 gallons | 9.8 – 52.6 L}*

Spec Racer Ford

The iRacing.com™ Spec Racer Ford (SRF) was released on April 28, 2009 and was well received for –above all else - its fun factor. The car just has a natural kind of feel you would expect from a small club racer. It has moderate amounts of power and grip which ramp up the required skill level for novices who are looking for a new challenge after the Solstice.

Spec Racer Ford events tend to be a mix of fun and frustration at times, depending on who is racing, since it is a car that may instill more confidence than the beginner driver can match with skill. As such, it is advised that any new SRF driver spend some quality time practicing with the car and finding appropriate setups once the basic feel of the car is understood.

Since most of the weight is in the rear of the car, but with same sized tires front and rear, the car has a unique feel which may take several laps to become accustomed to. Oversteer is the most common complaint, and as such the driver needs to develop good skills on the throttle and brake. Smoothness is paramount.

Specs

General

Style	Single-seater racecar
Drivetrain	Rear- engine, rear wheel drive

Tires

Brand	Goodyear Eagle A400 Spec Racer Ford
Size	22.0"x7.0" - 13"
Circumference	68.5" | *1.740 m*
Radius	10.9" | *0.277 m*
Construction	Radial (dry racing tire)
Tread	Slick with four longitudinal grooves
Wheel size	13"

Suspension, Steering & Brakes

Suspension	Independent front and rear; inboard shocks actuated by rocker arms; with adjustable sway bars front and rear
Steering	10.0: 1?
Steering Ratio	rack and pinion
Turns, Lock-to-lock	1.33
Brake type	Discs front and rear
Brake bias	Adjustable in setup
Braking aid	N/A

Engine

Specs	Ford, 1.9 Liter fuel-injected SOHC 8 valve Hemi-head 4 cylinder (inline), water cooled
Compression Ratio	9.0 : 1
Power	117 hp | *87.2 kW* @ 5300 RPM
Torque	135 ft-lb | *183 N-m* @ 4200 RPM
Weight : Power ratio	14.8 lb/hp | *8.96 kg/kW*
Power : Weight ratio	0.0677 hp/lb | *0.112 kW/kg*

Drivetrain

Transmission	5 speed manual
Differential	Open
Gear Ratios	
1st	3.42:1
2nd	1.84:1
3rd	1.29:1
4th	0.97:1
5th	0.77:1
Final Drive Ratio	3.62:1

Aero

CdA	6.72 ft^2 | *0.624 m^2*
Frontal Area	16.9 ft^2 | *1.57 m^2*
Drag coefficient, Cd	0.397

Dimensions

Weight in sim	1722 lb | *781 kg*
Weight Distribution F/R	38.4% / 61.6 %
Wheelbase	92.0" | *234 cm*
Track Width F/R	66" / 66" | *168 cm / 168 cm*
Height	43" | *109 cm*
Width	66" | *168 cm*
Length	147" | *373 cm*
Center of Gravity Height	17" | *43.2 cm* (approx)

Performance (using baseline setup)

Top Speed	126 mph | *203 kph* (no draft)
Skidpad Lateral acceleration	
50m | 165 ft	1.21 G (54.7 mph | *88.0 kph*)
150m | 492 ft	1.18 G (93.2 mph | *150 kph*)
Max Forward Acceleration	0.82 G
0 – 100 kph (62 mph)	5.63 s
Optimal Shift RPMs	
$1^{st} - 2^{nd}$	6100
$2^{nd} - 3^{rd}$	5800
$3^{rd} - 4^{th}$	5700
$4^{th} - 5^{th}$	5600
Braking	
100 – 50 kph	1.40 s
100 – 0 kph	2.62 s
161 – 0 kph	5.26 s
Max Deceleration	1.21 G

Page 60 — iRacing Paddock — Cars

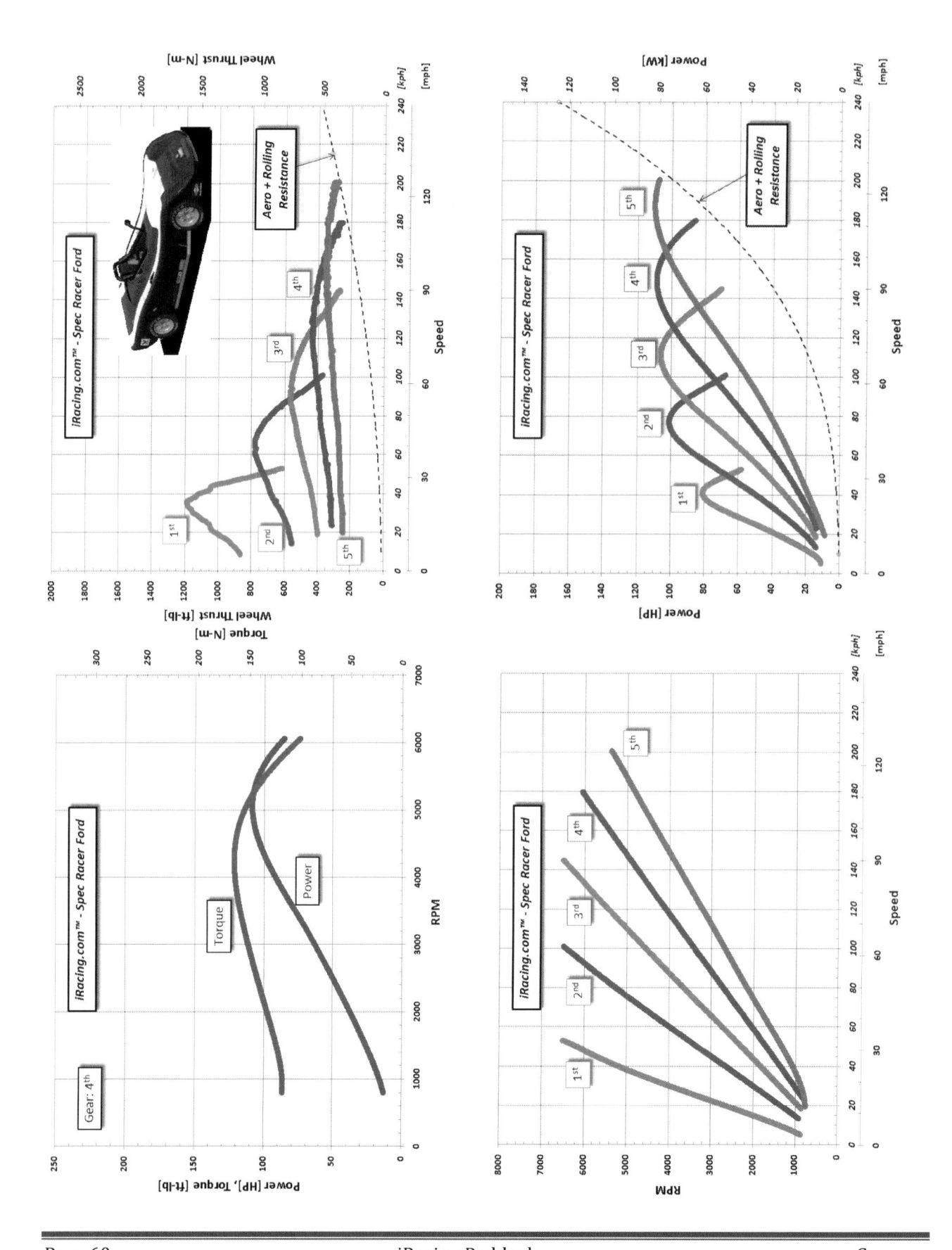

Baseline setup for Spec Racer Ford {range for each option}

Tire Pressures	
Front L/R	23.0 / 23.0 psi {16.0 – 40.1 psi} | *207/207 kPa {110 – 276 kPa}*
Rear L/R	22.5 / 22.5 psi {16.0 – 40.1 psi} | *207/207 kPa {110 – 276 kPa}*
Front Brake Bias	62.5% {45% - 75%}
Toe In	
Front	-1/32" {-19/32" - $^+$12/32"} | *-0.8 mm {-15.1 - $^+$9.5 mm}*
Rear	$^+$1/32" {-16/32" - $^+$16/32"} \| *$^+$0.8 mm {-12.7 - $^+$12.7 mm}*
Camber	
Front L/R	-1.1° / -1.1° {-4.5° - $^+$0.5° / -4.5° - $^+$0.5°}
Rear L/R	-1.5° / -1.5° {-4.3° - $^+$0.8° / -4.3° - $^+$0.8°}
Caster	
Left Front	$^+$4.4° {$^+$1.2° - $^+$7.2°}
Right Front	$^+$4.4° {$^+$1.2° - $^+$7.2°}
Rebound stiffness	
Front L/R	+10 clicks {0 – 20 clicks}
Rear L/R	+5 clicks {0 – 20 clicks}
Spring Perch	
Front L/R	5.875" {4.375 – 6.250"} | *14.9 cm {11.1 – 15.9 cm}*
Rear L/R	6.375" {5.000 – 6.750"} | *16.2 cm {12.7 – 17.1 cm}*
Ride Height	(adj. by spring perch settings; for information only)
Front L/R	3.16" {5.08 – 2.71"} | *8.03 cm {12.9 – 6.88 cm}*
Rear L/R	3.46" {5.09 – 3.02"} | *8.79 cm {12.9 – 7.67 cm}*
Anti Roll Bar	
Front	firm {soft – med - firm}
Rear	soft { soft – med - firm }
Fuel	no settings

Skip Barber F 2000

The Skip Barber F2000 is a car familiar to many who have attended Skip Barber racing schools in the United States. It is another great learning car as its rearward weight bias and open differential means it has a tendency to oversteer when pedal movements are too abrupt (beware of sudden oversteer if you come off the throttle very quickly). Thus it is a perfect car to teach good car control and help to develop good car control habits.

The best example is learning how to steer the car with the brake and throttle as much as with the steering wheel. Like anything this takes practice. The one notable odd feeling with this car is the very high gear ratio of first gear which means it pulls away from a stop very slowly until the revs come up.

Skip Barber events have frequently been the most popular and well-attended series in the whole service, and its popularity continues. Races tend to have enough splits to match drivers of similar skills and thus the races tend to be more enjoyable and challenging.

General

Style	Single-seat, open-wheel racecar
Drivetrain	Mid- engine, rear wheel drive

Tires

Brand	BF Goodrich g-Force
Size	225/50ZR16
Pressure	24 psi | *165 kPa*
Circumference	78.2" | *1.987 m*
Radius	12.45" | *0.316 m*
Construction	Radial (dry + wet tire)
Tread	Grooved tread with rain channels
Wheel size	16"

Suspension, Steering & Brakes

Front suspension	Fully independent
Rear suspension	Fully independent
Steering	Rack and pinion
Steering Ratio	9.0 : 1 ?
Turns, Lock-to-lock	1.25
Brake type	Discs front and rear
Brake bias	Adjustable in setup
Braking aid	N/A

Engine

Specs	2.0L SOHC 4-Cylinder
Compression Ratio	9.8 : 1
Horsepower	135 hp | *101 kW* @ 5600 RPM
Torque	135 ft-lb | *183 N-m* @ 4800 RPM
Weight : Power ratio	11.0 lb/hp | *6.66 kg/kW*
Power : Weight ratio	0.0910 hp/lb | *0.150 kW/kg*

Drivetrain

Transmission	Hewland LJS 5-Speed Sequential
Differential	Open
Gear Ratios	
1st	2.067:1
2nd	1.706:1
3rd	1.444:1
4th	1.182:1
5th	0.960:1
Final Drive Ratio	3.444:1

Aero

CdA	5.45 Ft^2 | *0.506 m^2*
Frontal Area	11.7 ft^2 | *1.09 m^2*
Drag coefficient, Cd	0.464

Dimensions

Weight in sim	1484 lb | *673 kg* (w/5.2 gallons of fuel)
Weight Distribution F/R	40.4% / 59.6%
Wheelbase	96.8" | *246 cm*
Track Width F/R	61.5" / 61.5" | *156 cm / 156 cm*
Height	41" | *104 cm*
Width	61.5" | *156 cm*
Length	144" | *366 cm*
Center of Gravity Height	14" | *36 cm* (approx.)

Performance (using baseline setup)

Top Speed	128 mph | *206 kph* (no draft)
Skidpad Lateral acceleration	
50m | 165 ft	1.19 G (54.1 mph | *87.1 kph*)
150m | 492 ft	1.15 G (92.0 mph | *148 kph*)
Max Forward Acceleration	0.44 G
0 - 100 kph (60 mph)	6.46 s
Optimal Shift RPMs	
$1^{st} - 2^{nd}$	6200
$2^{nd} - 3^{rd}$	6000
$3^{rd} - 4^{th}$	6100
$4^{th} - 5^{th}$	6300
Braking	
Max Deceleration	1.31+ G
100 – 50 kph	1.17 s
100 – 0 kph	2.50 s
161 – 0 kph	4.00 s

Cars — iRacing Paddock — Page 65

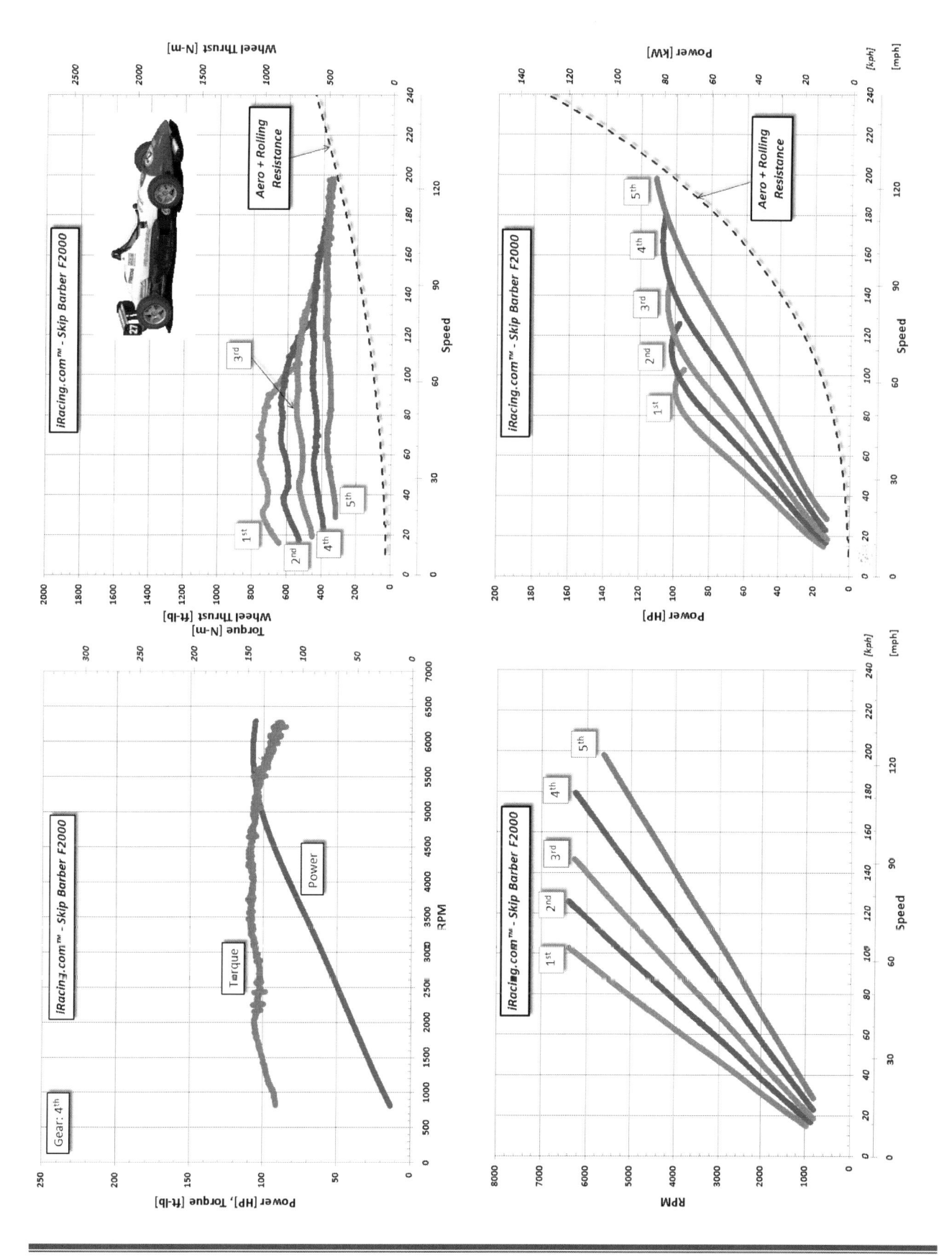

Baseline Setup {range for each option}

Tire Pressures	
Front L/R	24.0 / 24.0 psi {17.4 – 40.1 psi} | *165 / 165 kPa {120 – 276 kPa}*
Rear L/R	24.0 / 24.0 psi {17.4 – 40.1 psi} | *165 / 165 kPa {120 – 276 kPa}*
Front Brake Bias	59% {45% – 65%}
Spring Perch Offset	
Left Front	-10/16" | *-1.6 cm* {-10/16" - +10/16" | *-1.6 cm - +1.6 cm*}
Right Front	-10/16" | *-1.6 cm* {-10/16" - +10/16" | *-1.6 cm - +1.6 cm*}
Camber	*Note: only adjustable via spring perch*
Front L/R	-1.5° / -1.5° {-1.5° - -3.5°}
Rear L/R	-2.7° / -2.7°
Ride Height, F/R	*Note: only adjustable via spring perch and tire pressures*
Front	3.65" | *9.3 cm* {1.95 – 3.65" | *5.0 – 9.3 cm*}
Rear	2.84" | *7.2 cm* {2.68 – 3.00" | *6.8 – 7.6 cm*}
Rear Anti Roll Bar	1 {1 (soft) – 8 (stiff)}
Fuel	5.2 gal | *20 L* {1.7 – 5.2 gal | *6.5 – 20 L*}

VW Jetta TDi

The VW Jetta TDi turbo diesel was released within iRacing on August 12, 2009 as the first front-wheel drive car on the service, and was an instant hit with many drivers who relished the pure driving challenge of a fixed setup series. As an added incentive of the winner of the series in late 2009 (Wyatt Gooden) was offered a chance to earn a sponsored ride in the real life VW Jetta TDi Cup, making for a memorable series for all who participated.

The car has more torque available than any of the other beginner cars and the different feel to the car adds to its charm. It will also alarm newcomers that the shift RPMs are in the 4000s which is unusual for a racecar. The main driving difference compared to rear-wheel drive cars is that when you accelerate you lose grip on the front where the driving wheels are, so accelerating out of sharp turns has a different feel.

The significant forward weight bias also makes the car feel different from the others on the service. ABS brakes can help, but using ABS seems to lengthen braking distances a little compared to proper braking technique near the threshold.

General

Style	4 door sedan
Drivetrain	Front- engine, Front wheel drive

Tires

Brand	Pirelli PZero
Size	245/645 – 18
Circumference	18.9" | *2.004 m*
Radius	12.78" | *0.3245 m*
Construction	Radial, DH (dry racing tire; hard compound)
Tread	Slick
Wheel size	18"

Suspension, Steering & Brakes

Suspension	advanced multi-link fully independent race-tuned suspension
Steering	Power assist, rack and pinion
Steering Ratio	16.4 : 1
Turns, Lock-to-lock	2.7
Brake type	Discs front and rear
Brake bias	Slight forward bias
Braking aid	ABS w/electronic brake-force distribution (EBD)

Engine

Specs	2 liter, turbocharged inline 4 cylinder TDi diesel
Compression Ratio	18.5 : 1
Horsepower	173 hp | *129 kW* @ 4200 RPM
Torque	268 ft-lb | *363 N-m* @ 2300 RPM
Weight : Power ratio	13.2 lb/hp | *7.99 kg/kW*
Power : Weight ratio	0.076 hp/lb | *0.125 kW/kg*

Drivetrain

Transmission	six-speed, double-clutch, automatic DSG transmission
Differential	Electronic differential lock
Gear Ratios	
1st	4.04:1
2nd	2.37:1
3rd	1.56:1
4th	1.16:1
5th	0.85:1
6th	0.76:1
Final Drive Ratio	3.88:1

Aero

CdA	7.01 ft^2 | *0.651 m^2*
Frontal Area	22.6 ft^2 | *2.10 m^2*
Drag coefficient, Cd	0.31

Dimensions

Weight	2275 lb | *1031 kg*
Weight Distribution F/R	61% / 39%
Wheelbase	101.6" | *258 cm*
Track Width F/R	60.6" / 59.8" | *154 cm / 152 cm*
Height	57.5" | *146 cm*
Width	69.3" | *176 cm*
Length	179.1" | *455 cm*
Center of Gravity Height	22" | *56 cm* (approx.)

Performance

Top Speed	130 mph | *209 kph* (no draft)
Skidpad Lateral acceleration	
50m | 165 ft	1.14 G (52.8 mph | *85.0 kph*)
150m | 492 ft	1.13 G (91.3 mph | *147 kph*)
Max Forward Acceleration	0.66 G
0 – 100 kph (62 mph)	6.48 s
Optimal Shift RPMs	
$1^{st} - 2^{nd}$	4500
$2^{nd} - 3^{rd}$	4500
$3^{rd} - 4^{th}$	4500
$4^{th} - 5^{th}$	4500
$5^{th} - 6^{th}$	4500
Braking	
100 – 50 kph	1.45 s
100 – 0 kph	3.08 (ABS) … 2.95 s w/o lockup
161 – 0 kph	4.85 s
Max Deceleration	1.21 G

Page 70 — iRacing Paddock — Cars

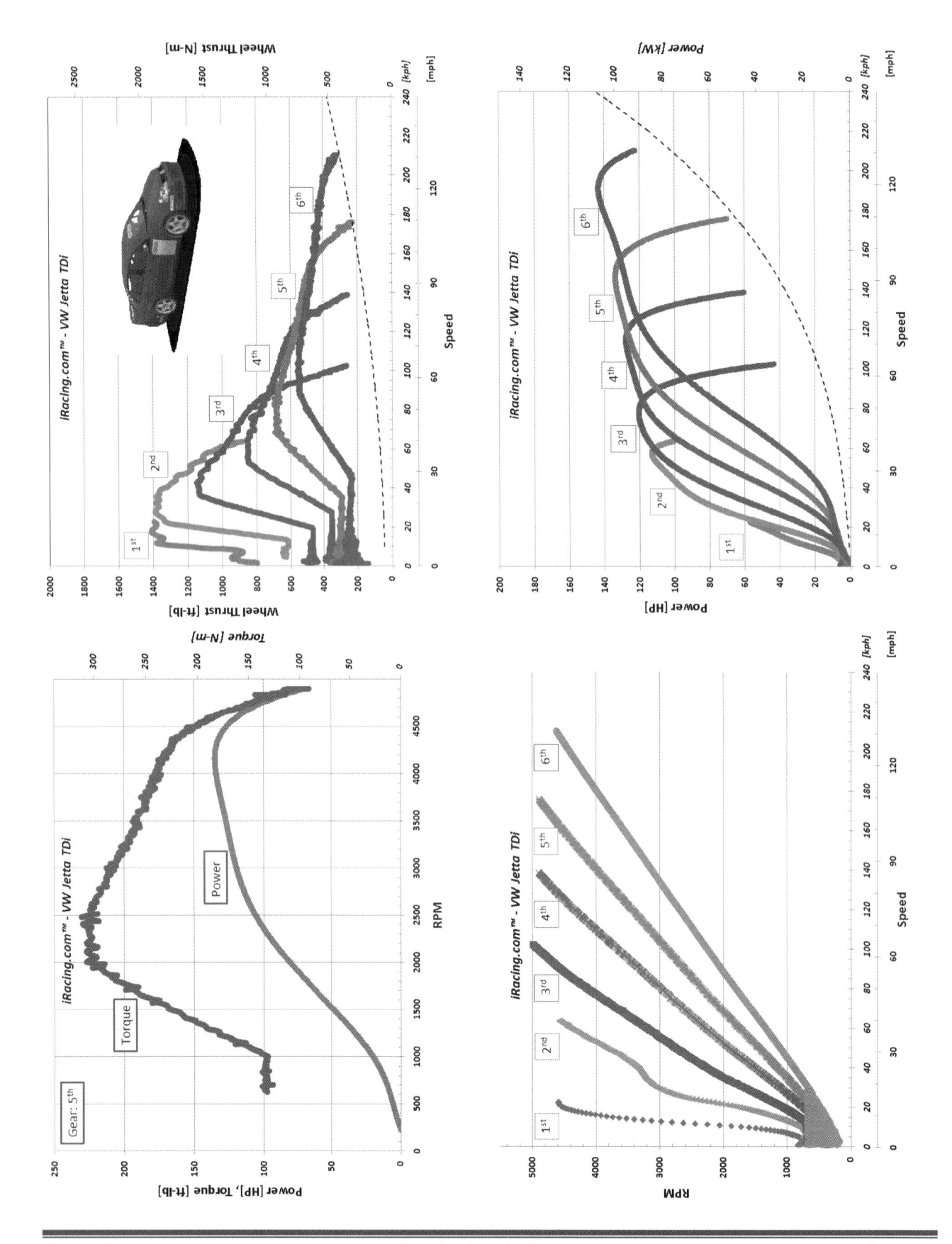

Setup

No setup options are available for the VW Jetta TDi car. The settings below are displayed on the setup page but are not adjustable.

Baseline Setup for VW Jetta TDi

Tire Pressures	
Front L/R	28.0 / 28.0 psi | *193 / 193 kPa*
Rear L/R	35.4 / 35.4 psi | *244 / 244 kPa*

Car Setup Guide

How to use the guide

First use a default setup and run some laps to determine how the car handles on the straights, turn entry, mid-corner, and exit. Then take note of the tire temperatures on the car setup window. Next, use the column headings to find the problems you noted and see if the corresponding rows with X's also describe the car feel and the diagnosis descriptions. If it looks like a change that will improve the situation, then apply the solution from the column on the right.

My general technique is to set front toe-in to one or two clicks below zero (minor toe out) and set rear toe to zero – then work on the proper tire pressures and camber settings first using the tire temperature readings and feel for the grip and handling behavior. Next, I will set the brake bias, and then work on anti-roll bar and toe settings to get the right balance. If I still struggle for handling and control, I will tweak the damper and spring perch settings.

Example - Spec Racer Ford:

Notes from a practice session: *Corner entry understeer (after braking), with corner exit oversteer. Temperatures of front tires look ok. Rear tire temperatures are about 10 F hotter on the inside edge. Middle temperatures of rear tires look to be close to the average of the inner and outer temperatures.*

Using the chart ... (see next page)
Corner entry understeer:
Tire pressure – based on tire temperatures front and rear pressures look to be ok; NO CHANGE ADVISED
Brake Bias – Decrease; understeer was noted after braking was completed; NO CHANGE ADVISED
Toe-in – Front – Decrease; a small amount of toe out helps turn in; POSSIBLE SOLUTION
Rebound – Front – Decrease; if car was overly responsive this would be worth trying; POSSIBLE SOLUTION
Rebound – Rear – Increase; if the car was overly sluggish this would be worth trying; POSSIBLE SOLUTION
Spring Perch Offset – Front – Increase; results in lower ride height in front; POSSIBLE SOLUTION
Spring Perch Offset – Rear – Decrease; results in higher ride height in rear; POSSIBLE SOLUTION
Anti-Roll Bar – Front – Decrease; should help with turn in; POSSIBLE SOLUTION

Corner exit oversteer:
Toe-in – Rear – Increase; a small amount of toe-in will help the car be stable on the straights but will feel very "understeery" – keep rear toe in close to zero unless all else fails; POSSIBLE SOLUTION
Rear Camber – Decrease; this also corresponds to the tire temperatures which appear to say that the camber is insufficient to spread the load across the tire during corning; GOOD SOLUTION
Rebound – Front – Decrease; if car was overly responsive this would be worth trying; POSSIBLE SOLUTION
Rebound – Rear – Increase; if car was overly sluggish this would be worth trying; POSSIBLE SOLUTION
Spring Perch Offset – Front – Decrease; opposite of recommendation for entry understeer. This solution should be left alone for the time being until other solutions are attempted. TRY LATER
Spring Perch Offset – Rear – Decrease; opposite of recommendation for entry understeer. This solution should be left alone for the time being until other solutions are attempted. TRY LATER
Anti-Roll Bar – Rear – Decrease; should help with getting the power down on exit; POSSIBLE SOLUTION

Summary of things to try first for this example situation:
- Rear Camber – Decrease
- Toe-in (front) – Decrease

... then do more laps to see if the corner entry understeer and corner exit oversteer were solved.

SPEC RACER FORD Setup Guide

SPEC RACER FORD Setup Guide			Corner Entry		Mid-corner		Corner Exit		Straights	Diagnosis	Feel	Solution
			Under steer	Over steer	Under steer	Over steer	Under steer	Over steer				
Tire Pressure*	Front		×	×	×	×	×	×		tire temp too low in center	Sluggish	Increase
			×	×	×	×	×	×		tire temp too high in center	Harsh	Decrease
	Rear		×	×	×	×	×	×		tire temp too low in center	Sluggish	Increase
			×	×	×	×	×	×		tire temp too high in center	Harsh	Decrease
Front Brake Bias				×						Rear tires lock prematurely	spins out w/ heavy braking	Increase
			×							Front locks up prematurely	no turn in w/ heavy braking	Decrease
Toe In	Front			×					Wanders	Reduced top speed if too far from zero	Toe-out (−) = sensitive at initial turn in	Increase but near 0
			×						Skittish, Unstable	Reduced top speed if too far from zero	Toe-in (+) = bad response to turn in	Decrease but near 0
	Rear					×		×	Unstable (esp. with toe out)	Reduced top speed if too far from zero	Snaps to oversteer	Increase but keep near 0
					×		×		Very stable with toe in	Reduced top speed if too far from zero	Pushes under power	Decrease but avoid toe out
Camber	Front									Inside edge of tire temp more than 20 F > than outer	Less braking capability	Increase
					×		×			Outside edge of tire temp > than inner	Less cornering grip	Decrease
	Rear									Inside edge of tire temp more than 20 F > than outer	Reduced acceleration	Increase
						×		×		Outside edge of tire temp > than inner	Less cornering grip	Decrease
Caster (affects front camber)									sensitive steering		Not enough feedback	Increase
									Bumps jar the wheel too much		Too much feedback; big effort to turn	Decrease
Rebound**	Front			×			×				Sluggish	Increase
			×					×			Touchy	Decrease
	Rear		×					×			Sluggish	Increase
				×							Touchy	Decrease
Spring Perch Offset (affects ride height)	Front		×		×		×				Car rolls a lot	Increase
				×		×		×	Bottoms out over bumps		Less cornering grip	Decrease
	Rear			×		×		×			Car rolls a lot	Increase
			×		×		×		Bottoms out over bumps		Less cornering grip	Decrease
Anti Roll Bar	Front			×						Slow response in esses and chicanes	Sluggish, but good feel; easy to recover	Increase
			×							Front tires hotter and wear faster; bumps upset the car	Touchy, fast response, less feel	Decrease
	Rear					×				Slow response in esses, chicanes	Sluggish but good feel; easy to catch	Increase
								×		Rear tires hotter and wear faster; bumps upset the car	Unstable with throttle mid-corner to exit	Decrease

Cars — iRacing Paddock — Page 73

Skip Barber F2000 Setup Guide

Skip Barber F2000 Setup Guide			Problem								Solution
			Corner Entry		Mid-corner		Corner Exit		Straights	Diagnosis	Feel	
			Under steer	Over steer	Under steer	Over steer	Under steer	Over steer				
Tire Pressure*	Front		×	×	×	×	×	×		tire temp too low in center	Sluggish	Increase
			×	×	×	×	×	×		tire temp too high in center	Harsh	Decrease
	Rear		×	×	×	×	×	×		tire temp too low in center	Sluggish	Increase
			×	×	×	×	×	×		tire temp too high in center	Harsh	Decrease
Front Brake Bias				×						Rear tires lock prematurely	spins out w/ heavy braking	Increase
			×							Front locks up prematurely	no turn in w/ heavy braking	Decrease
Spring Perch Offset (affects camber and ride height)			×		×		×			Inside edge of tire temp more than 20 F > than outer	Less braking capability	Increase
				×		×		×	Bottoms out over bumps	Outside edge of tire temp > than inner	Less cornering grip	Decrease
Anti Roll Bar	Rear					×				Slow response in esses, chicanes	Sluggish but good road feel; easy to "catch"	Increase
								×		Rear tires hotter and wear faster	Unstable with throttle mid-corner to exit	Decrease

Notes:

* Tire pressures need to be optimized. For example, if better optimized at the front than the rear, the car will tend to oversteer – but this will not determine whether the rear pressure will need to be increased or decreased. Examining the temperature of the middle of the tires in relation to the edges after a few warm-up laps is the best way to know whether to increase or decrease tire pressures. Conversely, you can dial in oversteer or understeer by intentionally missing the optimum pressure. For instance, many new drivers struggle with perceived oversteer in the Skip Barber car, and the advised solution is to increase the front tire pressure by as much as 3-8 psi more than the rears until the car understeers (easier for novices to control). Once the driver becomes more skilled, they can dial back the front pressure until it equates to the rear, which achieves the best grip and is thus the fastest setup.

** Damper rebound settings are more difficult to define since it will depend on the nature of the turn and the degree of acceleration (and load transfer). For instance, a fast turn without braking may not result in any weight transfer from the rear to the front which is completely different to a decreasing radius turn with turning and load transfer to front (trail braking) and to the outside or a tight turn where all the braking is done in a straight line, and thus corner entry has some rebound significance in the front. If the advice from the chart does not achieve the desired result, try going the other way on rebound settings to see if the turns in question have better results. Note also that rebound settings that help with understeer in entry may result in the opposite effect on exit, so the best setting is always a compromise.

Also note that a more detailed Setup Guide is provided by iRacing and the link is found on the iRacing member page under "Reference".

Car Comparison

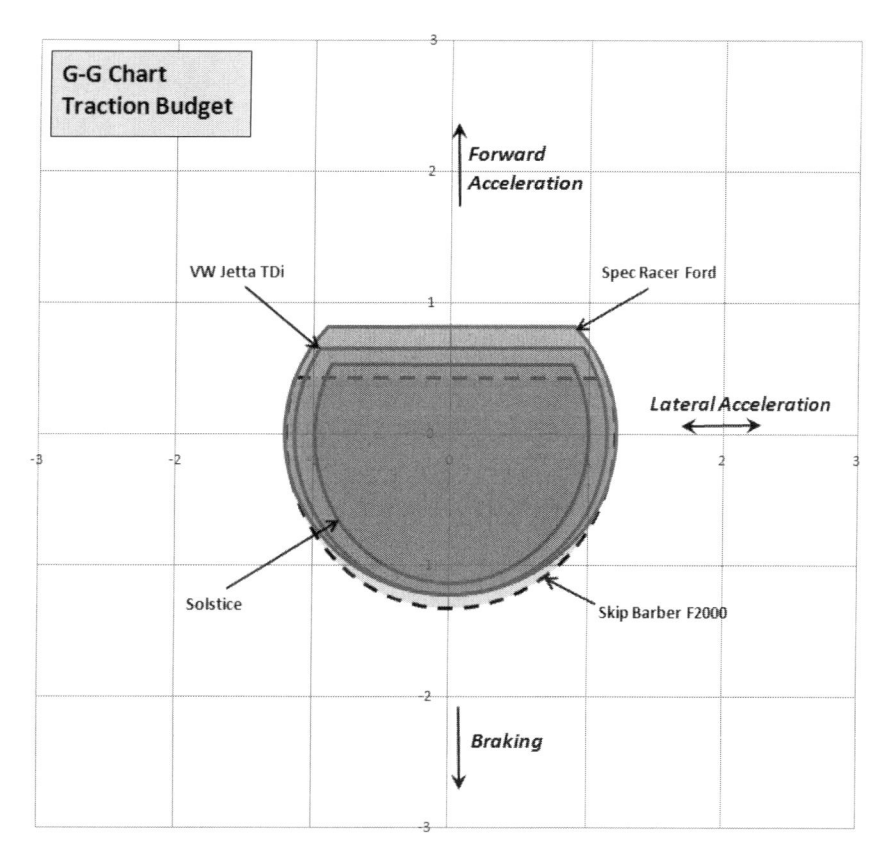

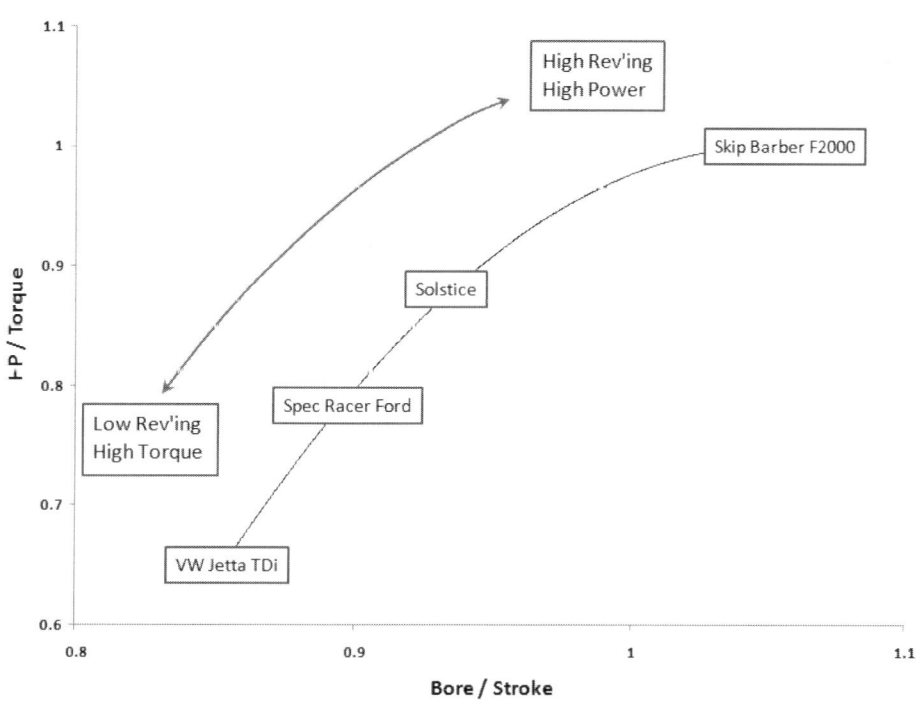

G-G Chart Traction Budget

- VW Jetta TDi
- Spec Racer Ford
- Solstice
- Skip Barber F2000

Forward Acceleration ↑
Lateral Acceleration ↔
Braking ↓

H-P / Torque vs **Bore / Stroke**

- High Rev'ing High Power
- Low Rev'ing High Torque
- Skip Barber F2000
- Solstice
- Spec Racer Ford
- VW Jetta TDi

Cars — iRacing Paddock — Page 75

iRacing.com™ Track Content

The tracks detailed in this book comprise all the road course content included with all iRacing subscriptions. Obviously this amounts to the tip of the iceberg, but for beginners it is advisable to focus on the fundamentals, and the included courses are a great cross section of tracks for learning. In fact, all are well known in real life as driving school tracks for the Skip Barber Racing School and other racing academies.

Each includes an iRacing aerial image of the entire circuit, a map showing its approximate location, and then the description (provided on iRacing's website), along with a driving description. This description was primarily written with the Skip Barber F2000 and the SRF in mind and is mainly to give beginners a simple walkthrough of the course and what to look out for. Most driving descriptions I have come across are excellent but are written by extremely fast drivers and as such the gear selections and braking points are often inappropriate for people just learning a new track. As a result, I have limited the amount of specific gear prescriptions and desired braking points, as they are very driver specific, and will evolve as the skill level changes. For the most part it is a simple list of things to watch out for as one completes a lap.

Another feature is a track map derived from an iRacing screenshot. You will notice that these pages are very uncluttered – this allows users to make copious notes about the track as they learn and perfect them. Driving schools all the way up to professional racers make use of track maps to point out problem areas and to guide the development of a setup. For beginners it may be enough to get oriented to the circuit and learn which way the track goes, but soon afterward it may be good to put down some notes about braking points, gear selection, optimal line, and so forth.

Most tracks also include a list of dimensions for the size of the turns (tight turns have smaller radius numbers and thus will require you to slow down more, while large radius turns can allow more speed to be carried through). Most of this data was obtained from on-track testing and is thus approximations of the true dimensions.

For fun I included some details about the real racetrack, should you want to research it more online – some tracks have useful information on their sites such as driving descriptions or helpful tips - or look to contact them for track days or racing school information. But this table also includes some iRacing specific details, like altitude (which affects the power of the engine and the aerodynamics), and the number of laps required to record an official TT session.

Additionally, there is a table which provides the existing world records for each of the cars from the book – but keep in mind this is only to show what fast laps are possible – changes in each build make the performance and handling different over time, so it may be unfair to put too much emphasis on current records. One metric people often use to benchmark rookie performance is to achieve a time within 107% of the track record, so those times are included as well. Finally, a non-scientific review of several rookie or D level races at each track provided a range of average lap times that the drivers finishing well would normally achieve. If you can consistently achieve the range of times shown then you will probably be very successful in rookie level races. If you are safe and consistent, but slower than those times, you may still finish very well, given the number of drivers who have incidents and lose time to do repairs (resets).

Lime Rock Park

Description (From iRacing.com)

"Nestled at the foot of the Berkshire Mountains in the Northwest corner of Connecticut, Lime Rock Park is as picturesque for visitors as it is challenging for drivers. At a relatively short 1.53 miles in length, its layout is deceptively simple. Even professional drivers find it difficult to unlock the secret of a very fast lap.

"Racers sometimes refer to its seven corners – six right-handers and one left – as a road racing short track due to the high average speed and the fact that there is no opportunity to relax during a lap.

"Opened on April 20, 1957, Lime Rock Park is the home track for the Skip Barber Racing School and is one of the oldest continuously-operated road courses in North America. The track has witnessed epic battles among some true legends of the sport. Drivers like Mark Donohue, Brian Redman, Hans Stuck, Paul Newman and Geoff Brabham have all battled their way to victory at Lime Rock Park.

"In addition to SCCA club races, Lime Rock Park hosts rounds of the American Le Mans Series in July (on a second track layout that utilizes a chicane just after the daunting Uphill corner) and the Grand Am GT series over the Memorial Day weekend. The track also is host annually to the NASCAR Camping World East Series."

Lime Rock Park: Driving Summary

Turn one (known as "Big Bend") is approached in top gear and requires hard braking. As you approach the turn in point, downshift into third while trail-braking (slow transition from braking to acceleration while approaching the apex). Many like to diamond this turn by doing two apexes one near the turn in and the other close to the exit. I tend to try to hug the apex all the way through the turn and ease on to the throttle smoothly. Carrying as much speed through the turn will win you some time, but is not as important as other parts of the track in terms of lap time.

Turn two will require you to brake heavier and earlier than you want because in order to gain enough time on the backstretch, you need to set up for turn three, and that means you need to be on the far left of the track at the exit of turn two. By sacrificing a perfect line in turn two you set up to gain time as you accelerate all the way through turn three. If you are too aggressive going through turn three you may clip the curb or just push off the track at the exit which is a deadly mistake.

For the Uphill Corner, brake lightly just as you pass the flag stand to help the car turn in. You can also accomplish this by easing off the throttle, but I find a light tap of the brakes will do the same. Turn in early in order to rotate the car and thus allow the car's momentum to swing wide and finish the turn as you crest the hill. When you lose grip over the crest, if your momentum is still sliding you sideways, you will need a fast correction to save it once the weight comes back onto the front tires. Make sure you pull the car away from the curb at the exit in order not to get an incident point for being off-track.

West Bend is a straight-forward 90 degree turn, followed by a dive downhill approaching the final turn. Many experienced drivers take this final turn flat out, but I find easing off the throttle a tiny bit during turn-in allows a much better chance of getting through it cleanly. You can gain time by not lifting, but occasionally you may have to scrub off speed to stay under control at the exit. Over the course of a race it is better to complete the turn reliably and close to maximum exit speed rather than going flat out and getting it wrong occasionally.

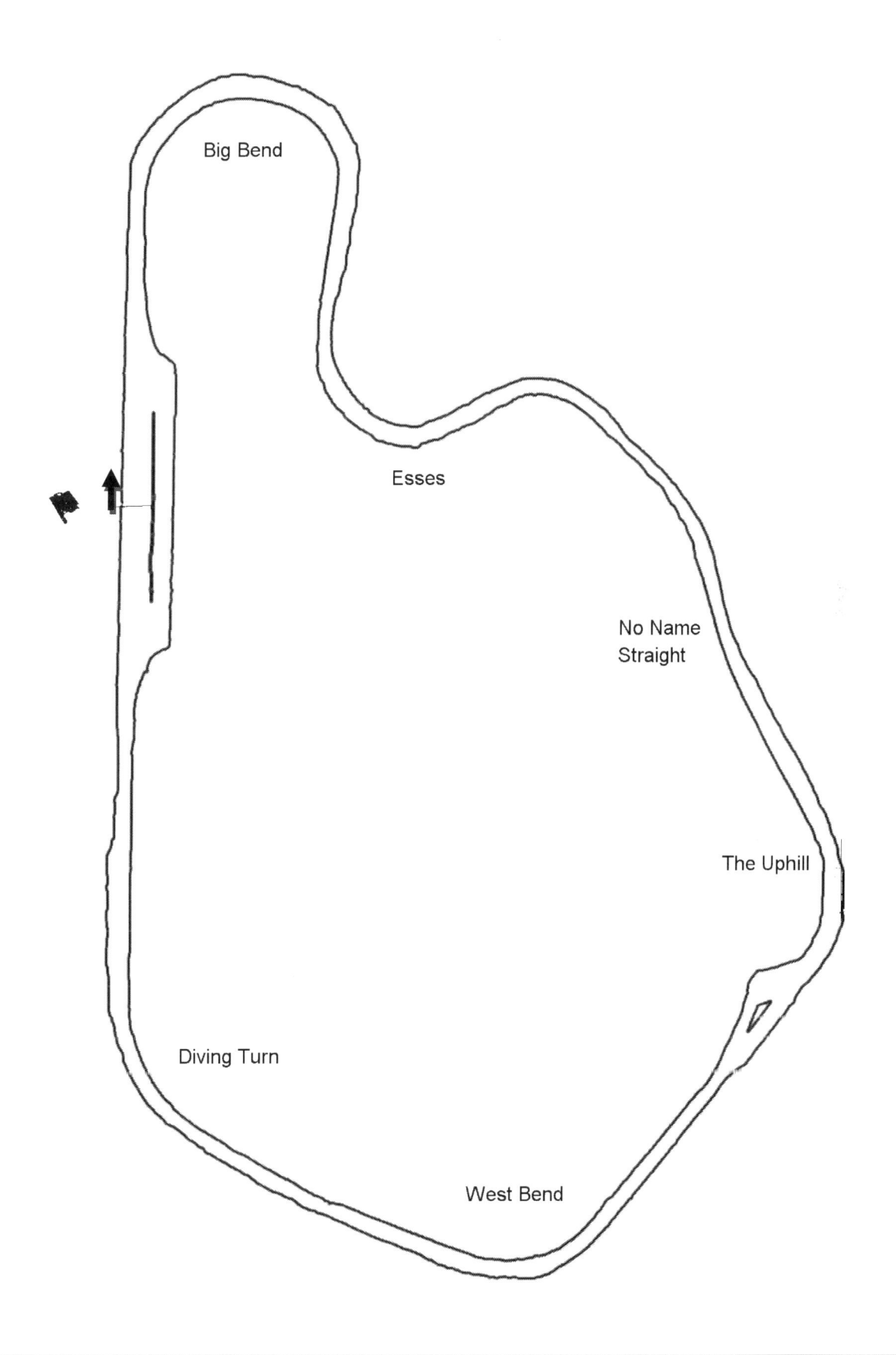

- Big Bend
- Esses
- No Name Straight
- The Uphill
- Diving Turn
- West Bend

Lime Rock Park – Vital Statistics

Track Name	Lime Rock Park
Location	Lakeville, CT, USA
Website	http://www.limerock.com
Contact Names	Cathy Glasner (Office Mgr); cathy@limerock.com
	Skip Barber (President and Owner)
	Georgia Blades (CEO); georgia@limerock.com
Important Events	Grand-Am (w/Daytona Prototypes), ALMS, Historic Festival, SCCA
Main Gate Address	60 White Hollow Road, Lakeville, CT 06039
Mailing Address	497 Lime Rock Road, Lakeville, CT 06039
Phone	(860) 435-5000	(800) 722-3577 (toll free)
Fax	(860) 435-5010
Time Zone	EST/EDT (GMT -0500/-0400)
Latitude, Longitude	41.927688° N, 73.383599° W
Altitude [m]	598 ft	182 m
# Turns	7 (6R, 1L)
Distance	1.54 mi	2.462 km (Full course), 1.54 mi	2.478 km (Chicane layout)
Laps for Time Trial (TT)	8 (both configurations)

Track Element	Length; Minimum Radius [ft	m]
S/F Straight	1903	580
T1 "Big Bend"	246	75
Straight	295	90
T2 "Esses"	197	60
Straight	85	26
T3 "Esses"	197	60
T4	394	120
"No Name Straight"	1033	315
T5 "Uphill"	279	85
Back Straight	761	232
T6 "West Bend"	295	90
Straight	646	197
T7 "Diving Turn"	394	120

Car	iRacing World Record	107%	Typical Rookie Race Lap time
Pontiac Solstice (R)	1:01.857 (G. Huttu)	1:06.187	1:07 – 1:10
Spec Racer Ford	58.298 (F. Hermann)	1:02.379	1:02 – 1:03
Skip Barber F2000	57.860 (C. Rondeico)	1:01.910	1:02 – 1:04
VW Jetta TDi	59.638 (W. Gooden)	1:03.813	1:01 – 1:03

Mazda Raceway Laguna Seca

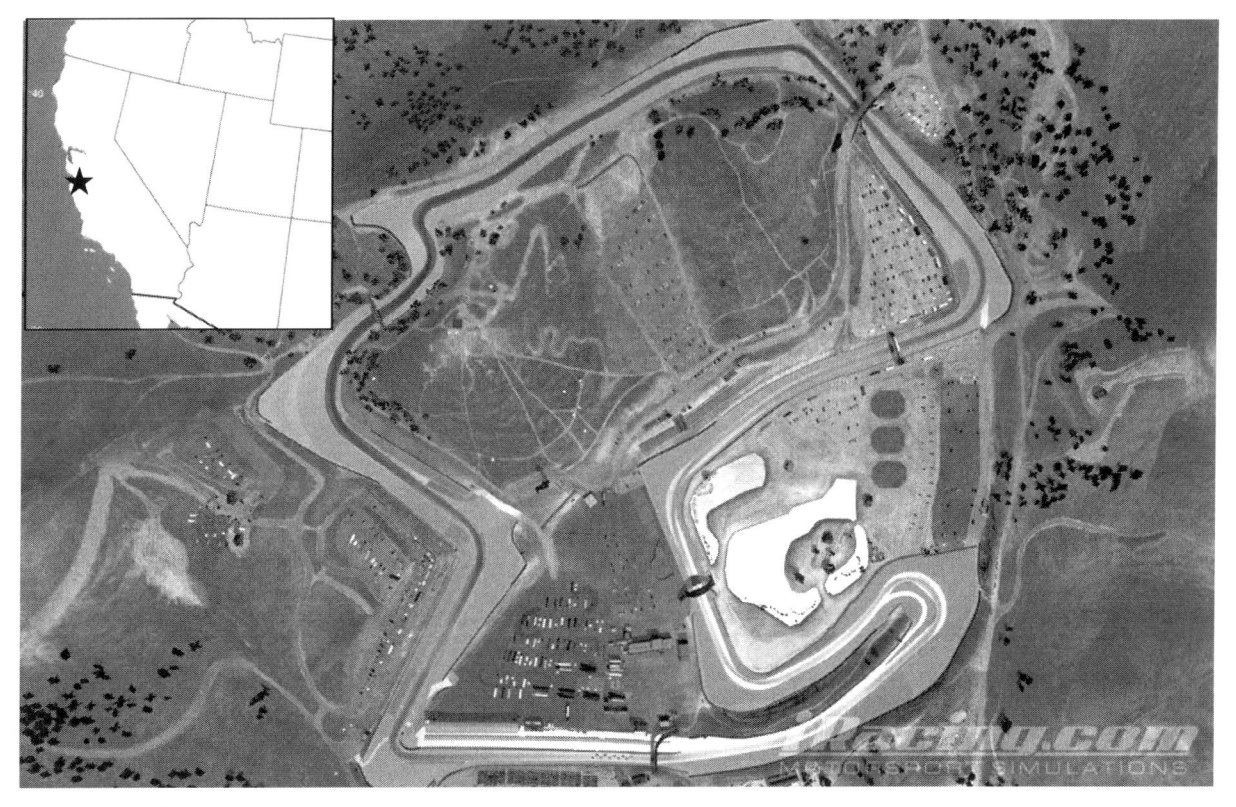

Description (from iRacing.com)

"Mazda Raceway Laguna Seca is one of the classic North American road-racing circuits. A serpentine ribbon of pavement winding through the hills of Northern California's Monterey Peninsula, "Laguna" is the site of one of the most unique and famous corners in motorsport – The Corkscrew. Approached from a long, fast uphill run, the Corkscrew is a blind, plunging lefthander that is more akin to a ski slope than a piece of race track.

"Originally built by the Army Corps of Engineers on a corner of what was then Fort Ord, Laguna Seca opened in 1957 and in its half century of operation has been host to every significant North American road-racing series, from the legendary Can-Am to the Trans-Am, IMSA Camel GT, and CART Indy cars. Today a part of the Monterey County park system, Mazda Raceway Laguna Seca hosts the Grand-Am Rolex Sports Car Series™, American Le Mans Series, Rolex Monterey Historic Automobile Races and is the West Coast home of the Skip Barber Racing School. In addition, the track hosts two of America's most important motorcycle races, the Red Bull U.S. Grand Prix, a round of the MotoGP World Championship and the Corona AMA Superbike Finale, the final round in America's premier motorcycle road-racing series."

Mazda Raceway Laguna Seca: Driving Description

Note: With the exception of turn eight (the 'Corkscrew'), every turn has a red-block at the apex just over the curbing. If you use too much curb at the apex and hit the block, you will upset the car and likely spin or have to slow down quite a bit in order to avoid spinning. Therefore, one should use all the curbing at most turns, but do not risk over-doing it as it will cost a lot of time.

Turn one is flat out and is simply a kink along the front stretch which crests a hill past the pits. The proper line is as far to left as possible and then wash out at the exit to the far right under heavy braking for the turn two Andretti hairpin. Bleed off enough speed to bring the car to first gear for an early and a second late apex, then smoothly transition to full throttle and bring the car back to the left side to prepare for turn three.

Turn three requires slower entry speed than it looks, best done with some trail braking, but once the front end bites, you can begin to bring back the throttle. Turn four is a simple right hander that needs a little braking and /or easing off the throttle to aid the turn in. It is crucial to have a good line going from curb to apex to curb to carry as much speed as possible down to the next left.

The next three corners will define the success or failure of a good lap. Turn five is at the base of a long hill, and thus carrying as much speed as possible is critical. Use the brake markers on the right to be consistent and trail brake to bring the front around. Once the weight transfer is complete you can coast a tiny bit until the apex where you can bring on full throttle and swing out wide toward the rumble strip on the right edge.

Turn six is even more tricky, as it is a deceptive kink which requires a little easing off of the throttle or a tap of the brake at the turn in point to prepare for a correctly lined up apex. Then it's back to full throttle, which is again very critical going up the rest of the long uphill straight towards turn seven which is the fast right just before the Corkscrew.

Turn eight is the left-right corkscrew which dives down the side of a steep hill. I tend to brake heavily as I hit the curbing on the right edge (apex of turn seven) and bring it down to first gear, but as soon as I'm sure the car will rotate into the left apex I upshift to second and roll onto full throttle going down the hill.

Turn nine should be started from the right side of the track and requires a little time off the throttle to allow the front end to bite and pull the car toward the apex, but be careful not to use too much right hand curb at the exit as the car may easily spin. Pull the car back to the left and brake early and downshift for the turn ten right hander. If you set it up well you can get back onto full throttle early, but the topography of the track can result in a loss of control if you are too aggressive, so be prepared to gently ease off if necessary.

The final turn can be tricky if you are impatient. Once you bleed off some speed to make the apex, roll back onto the throttle gently so that you avoid using too much exit curbing which can also cause a spin.

Tracks   iRacing Paddock   Page 83

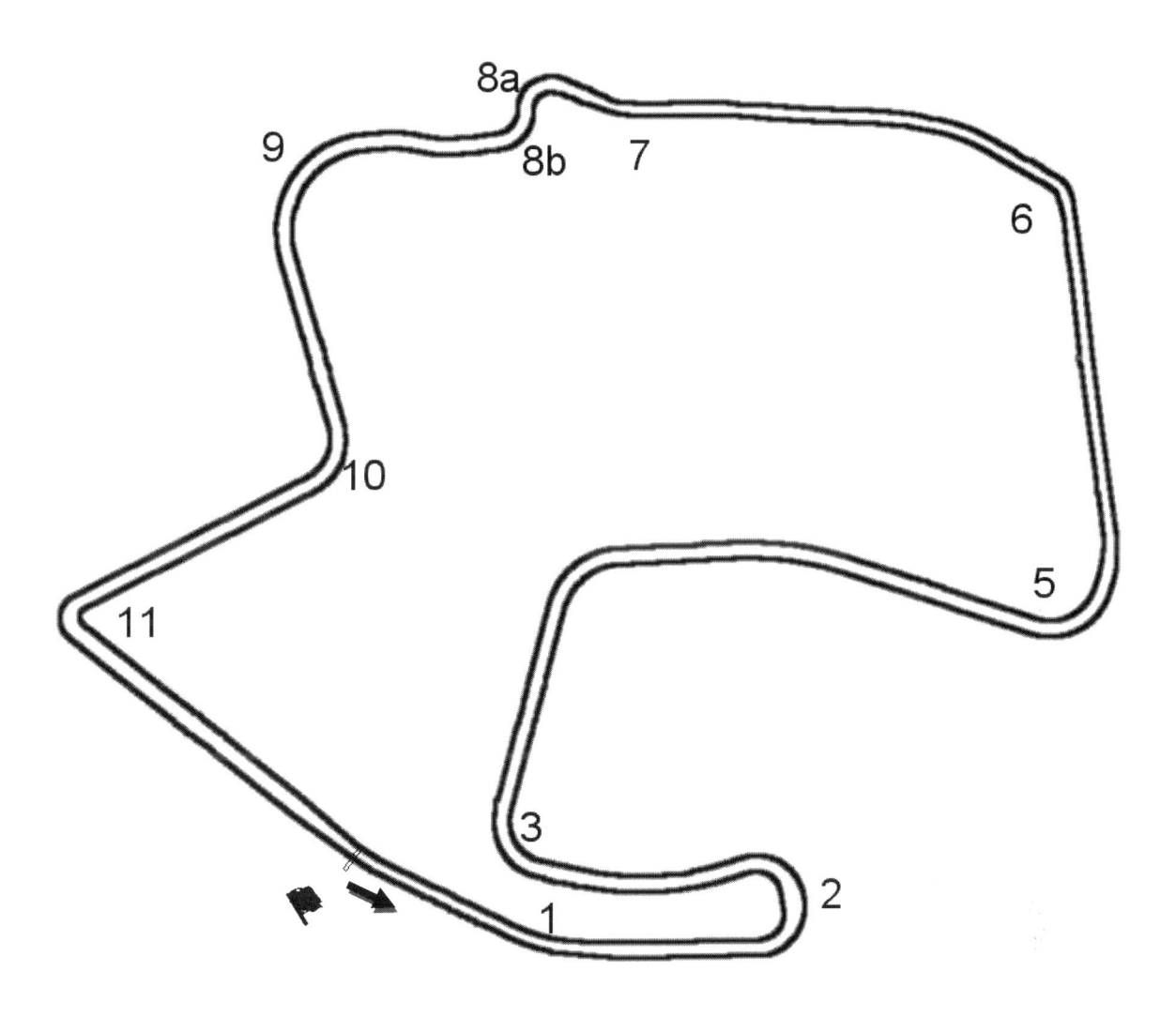

Mazda Raceway Laguna Seca – Vital Statistics

Track Name	Mazda Raceway Laguna Seca
Location	Monterey, CA, USA
Website	http://www.mazdaraceway.com/
Contact Names	Jennifer Capasso, PR: Jennifer@MazdaRaceway.com
Important Events	ALMS, MotoGP, Monterey Motorsports Reunion (Historics)
Address	1021 Monterey-Salinas Highway, Salinas, CA 93908
Phone	(831) 242-8201	(800) 327-7322 (toll free)
Time Zone	PST/PDT (GMT -0800/-0700)
Latitude, Longitude	36.584722° N, -121.752778° W
Altitude [m]	749-929 ft	228 - 283 m
# Turns	11 (7L, 4R)
Distance	2.24 mi	3.602 km
Laps for Time Trial (TT)	4

Track Element	Length; Minimum Radius [ft	m]
S/F Straight	1485	452
T1	517	158
Straight	342	104
T2 "Andretti Hairpin"	127	39
Straight	162	49
T3	145	44
Straight	629	192
T4	200	61
Straight	1325	404
T5	170	52
Straight	990	302
T6	180	60
"Rahal Straight"	1265	385
T7	450	137
T8a "Corkscrew entry"	75	23
T8b "Corkscrew exit"	90	27
Straight	416	127
T9 "Rainey Curve"	265	81
Straight	527	161
T10	150	46
Straight	799	243
T11	45	14

Car	iRacing World Record	107%	Typical Rookie Race Lap time
Pontiac Solstice (R)	1:45.550 (H.Luis)	1:52.939	1:56 – 2:00
Spec Racer Ford	1:39.324 (R.Towler)	1:46.277	1:46 – 1:50
Skip Barber F2000	1:37.835 (M.Dell'Orco)	1:44.683	1:42 – 1:46
VW Jetta TDi	1:41.088 (M.Dell'Orco)	1:48.164	1:44 – 1:46

Summit Point Raceway – Main Course

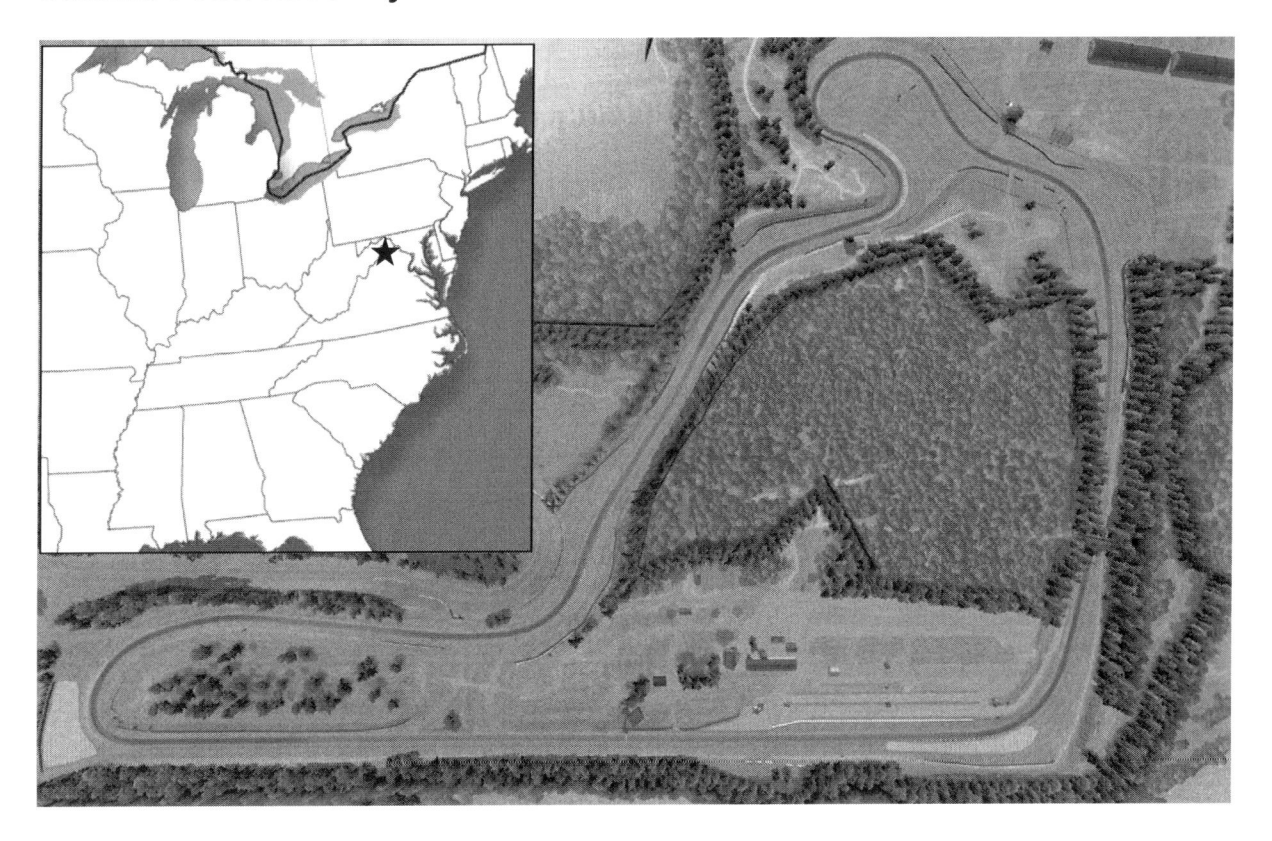

Description (from iRacing.com)

"With the hilly but high-speed 2 mile Summit Point track (in full and short versions) and the 1.1 mile highly technical Jefferson Circuit, Summit Point Motorsports Park offers every challenge a road-racer could desire – and then some.

"Set in the lush West Virginia countryside just over the border from Northern Virginia and less than two hours from Washington, DC, driving any of the Summit Point circuits is like a very fast tour over country roads. Summit Point opened in 1973 and while early in its history the track hosted professional road-racing series, in recent years the focus for the entire facility has been on amateur racing, high-performance driver training and club events.

"The Summit Point circuit, in either its long or short configuration, is quite fast and features a 40-foot elevation change. The 2,900-foot pit straight is preceded by a fast right-hander, so speeds are high at the braking point for the acute corner at the end of the straight. Miss your braking point and you'll have a fast trip through tall grass. The fast downhill approach to the tight Wagon Wheel also requires careful and precise braking on the approach and careful throttle modulation all the way around the long corner.
"The Jefferson Circuit is a great learning tool, with seven turns – lefts, rights, switchbacks and elevation changes – crammed into barely more than a mile of pavement."

Summit Point Raceway – Main Course: Driving Description

Approaching turn one, brake hard, downshift to second (some prefer first but I find second will allow for better control of oversteer when you exit) and hold some trail braking during turn in but release the brake as you approach the apex. As the radius widens at the exit, you can swing out a little, but I have found it best to hold tight onto the right until near the end of the turn (which is at that point called turn two).

Turn three requires perfect timing and good feel for weight transfer. You will need to ease onto the brakes and downshift a gear which will permit the car to turn in and then you may coast until the apex at which point you can quickly but smoothly get back onto the throttle for the twisty lead up to turn four.

Turn four can be taken flat out, but beginners may find it easier to ease off the throttle a tiny bit to aid in control. But be aware of drivers following close behind who may not expect you to bleed off speed at that point. You have to turn in early to get the line just right. Do not worry about your exit line from turn four.

Many fast people end up at the far left edge of the track which is not the best set-up for the following hairpin left. However, the time gained by going flat out on turn three will make up for any inefficiency there.

As you finish turn four get hard onto the brakes when your steering wheel is straight and downshift quickly down to second gear and eventually first while holding heavy straight-line braking. Any steering corrections while braking heavily will result in a loss of control here.

Be very gentle on the throttle in the hairpin as the rear end will be easy to spin around if you apply too much. You will be tempted to upshift before the next turn, but that would be a waste as you would need to downshift again a split second later. Hold minimal throttle corrections though turn six until you have enough room at the exit to bring up full acceleration before the exit. Maintain full throttle though the next two turns if you have practiced the line. If you are beginning, just ease off the throttle when entering each until you gain experience and confidence.

The final turn is a tricky one to get right and requires lots of practice. The best advice is to go slower than you think you need to until you can be consistent and then try to carry a little more speed each time. I brake moderately as I'm passing the pit lane entry point and drop it down a gear and then coast as the car turns in. When I'm confident I can get the apex and exit lined up, I bring the throttle back on as quickly and smoothly as I can.

Tracks   iRacing Paddock   Page 87

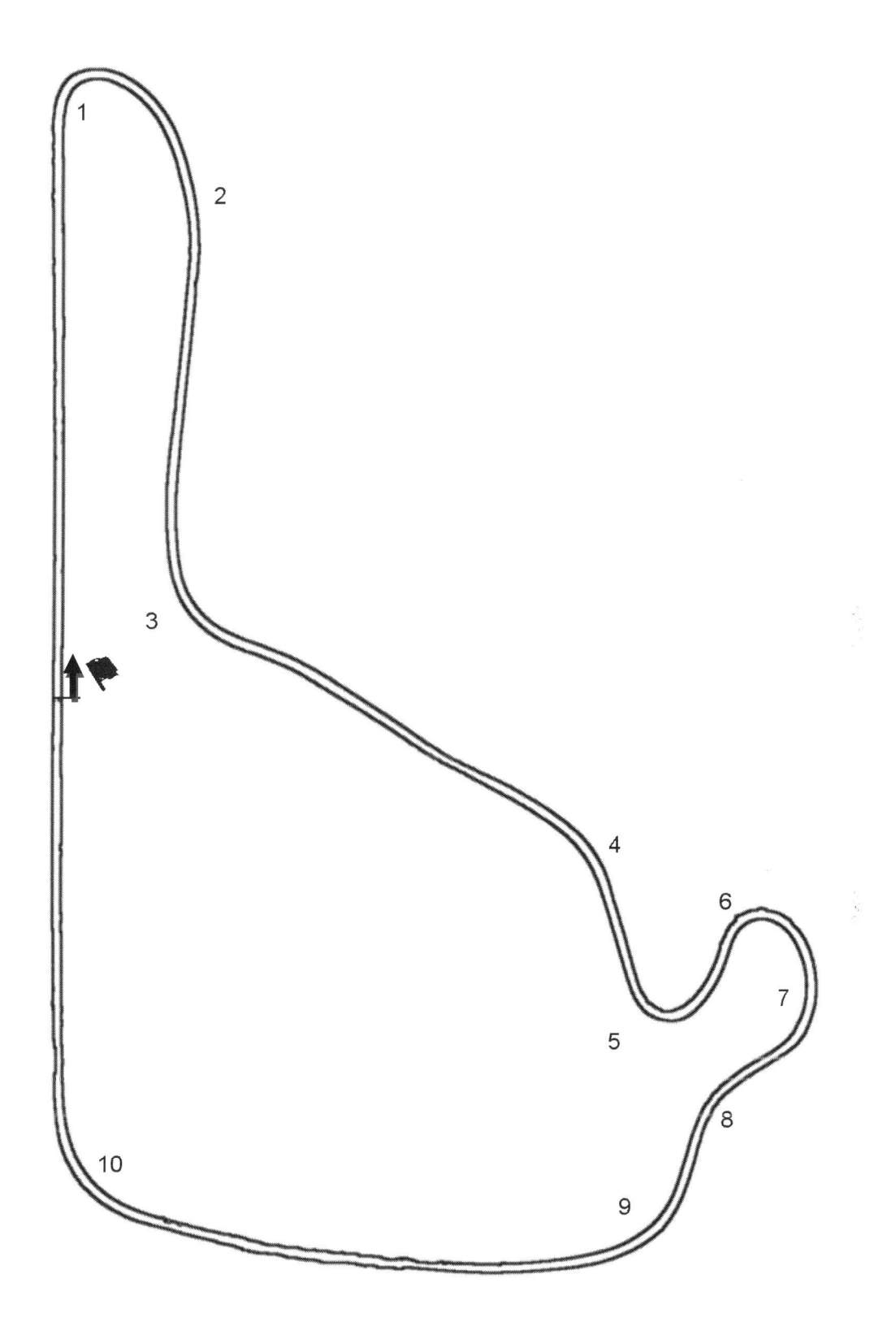

Summit Point Raceway – Main Course: Vital Statistics

Track Name	Summit Point Raceway
Location	Summit Point, WV
Website	http://www.summitpoint-raceway.com
Main Gate Address	Route 13 (Summit Point Road), Summit Point, WV, USA 25446
Mailing Address	PO Box 190 Summit Point, WV 25446
Phone	(304) 725-8444
Fax	(304) 728-7124
Latitude, Longitude	39.23439° N, -77.97529° W
Altitude	626 ft | 191 m
# Turns	10 (7R, 3L; Main layout)
	9 (6R, 3L; Short layout)
Distance	1.98 mi | 3.187 km (Main layout)
	1.46 mi | 2.35 km (Short layout)
Laps for Time Trial (TT)	7 (Main layout)
	8 (Short layout)

Track Element	Length; Minimum Radius [ft | m]
S/F Straight	2657 | 810
T1	125 | 38
T2	460 | 140
Straight	555 | 169
T3	285 | 87
Straight	738 | 225
T4	590 | 180
Straight	262 | 80
T5 Left Hairpin	114 | 34
Straight	66 | 20
T6 Right Hairpin	105 | 32
T7	260 | 80
T8	290 | 90
Straight	144 | 44
T9	340 | 105
Straight	1230 | 375
T10	350 | 107

Car	iRacing World Record	107%	Typical Rookie Race Lap time
Pontiac Solstice	1:27.300 (G.Huttu) – non Rookie version	1:33.411	1:29 – 1:32
Spec Racer Ford	1:21.354 (R.Burke)	1:27.049	1:26 – 1:29
Skip Barber F2000	1:20.826 (C.Aranha)	1:26.484	1:24 – 1:27
VW Jetta TDi	1:21.319 (C.Modoff)	1:27.011	1:25 – 1:27

Summit Point Raceway – Short Course

Summit Point Raceway – Short Course Driving Description

Near the start/finish line you will need to get hard onto the brakes and be careful not to trail-brake too aggressively, as the change in camber can upset the car through turn one. Hold the car to the right through the double apex turn and then straighten out the next turn by touching the curbs on the left and at the exit on the right. The rest of the lap is identical to the description of the Main Course starting at "turn four" (which amounts to turn three in this layout).

iRacing World Records:
Solstice = 1:09.451 (E.Foss)
Spec Racer Ford= 1:04.150 (E.Erlekotte)

Rookie Typical Race Lap
Solstice: 1:13 – 1:16
Spec Racer Ford: 1:08 – 1:10

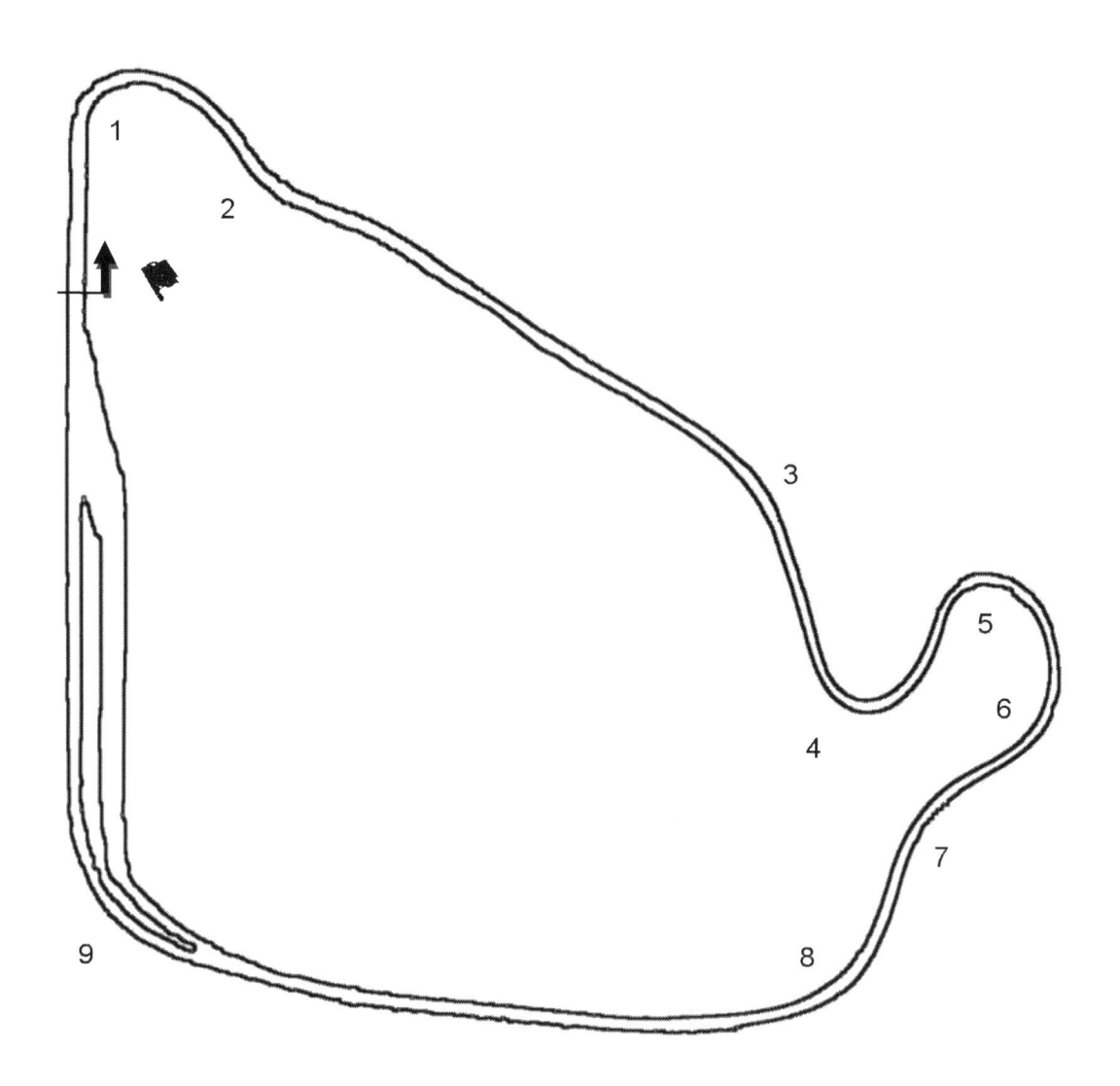

Summit Point Raceway – Jefferson Circuit

Jefferson Circuit: Driving Description

At the end of the main straight brake hard for turn one – trail braking in this spot is an asset to a fast lap. Resist the urge to punch the throttle once you approach the apex, as the turn is a long one. Ease back onto the throttle as you wind through the next two turns, going up a couple gears in the process. Again hard braking for turn four on the right edge of the track and then do your best to hold to the left all the way around until the exit (Turn 5).

There is a short downhill straight and a short dab of the brakes will set the car up for the fast left. It's ok to start from the far right, but make you way across to the left before the apex, as the negative camber from the crown of the road will work against you. Once you are sure to hit the apex with a good line toward the exit, you can bring on throttle very quickly to accelerate down the back straight. A very soft right hand kink leads to heavy braking for the final turns (eight and nine). Carrying too much speed here is a deadly mistake. Always err on the side of caution and slow down more than you think you need to, that way you can be ready to bring on full throttle when the tire grip is ready. The fastest way I've found through 8 and 9 is to hug the left edge from the middle of turn 9 until the exit, although a diamond approach can work also (early and late apex, swinging out wide in the middle of the turns). Be careful not to use too much curb on the exit as it will result in a big bump which can disrupt getting the power down.

Tracks　　　　　　　　　iRacing Paddock

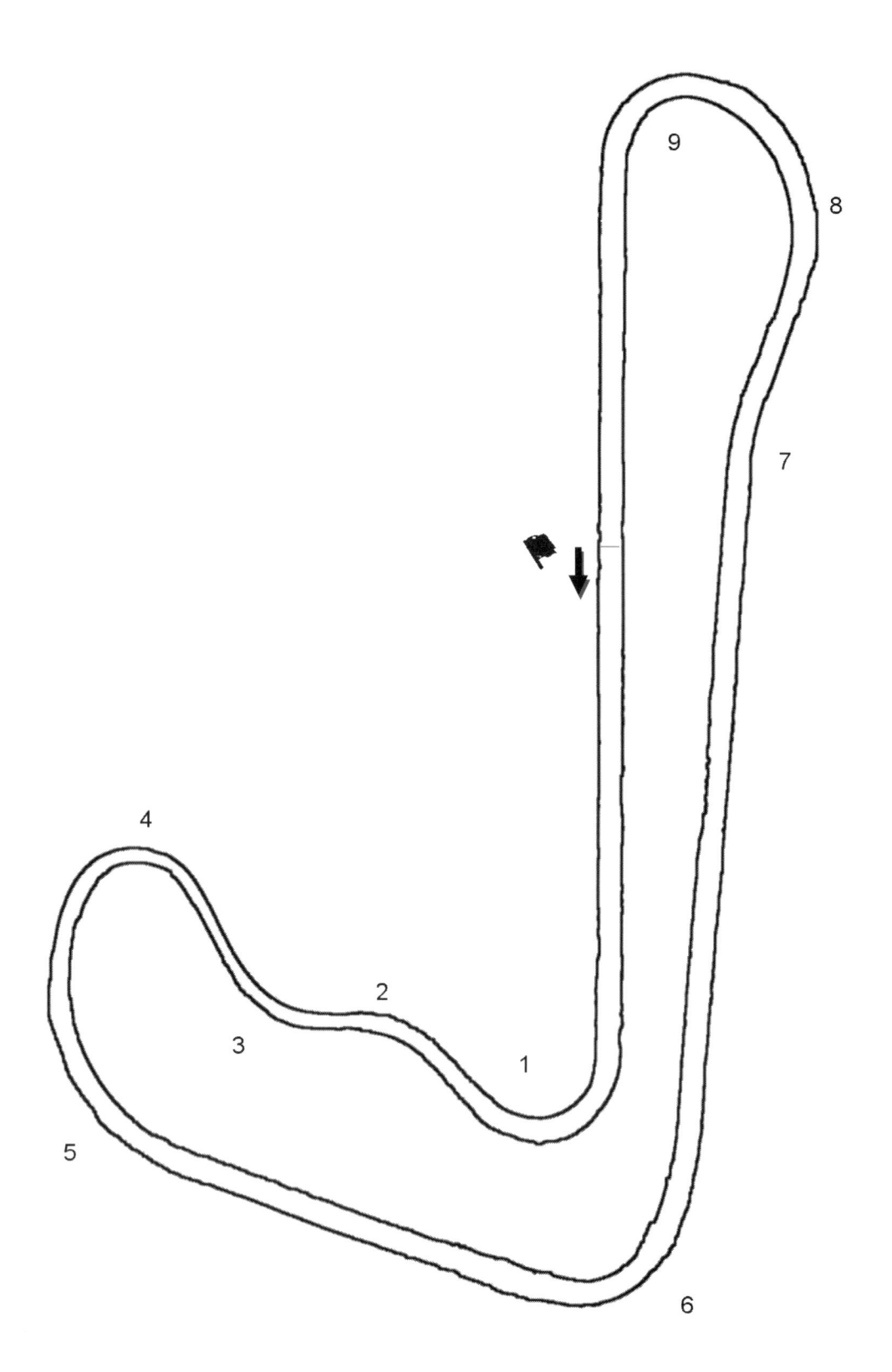

Summit Point Raceway – Jefferson Course: Vital Statistics

Track Name	Summit Point Raceway – Jefferson Circuit
Location	Summit Point, WV
Altitude	626 ft | 191 m
# Turns	9 (3L, 6R; Jefferson)
	9 (6R, 3L; Jefferson Reverse)
Distance	1.11 mi | 1.786 km (both directions)
Laps for Time Trial (TT)	8 (both directions)

Track Element	Length; Minimum Radius [ft | m]
S/F Straight	1171 | 357
T1	118 | 36
T2	161 | 49
T3	177 | 54
T4	89 | 27
T5	272 | 83
Straight	538 | 164
T6	151 | 46
Straight	748 | 228
T7	1312 | 400
Straight	115 | 35
T8	164 | 50
T9	91 | 28

Car	iRacing World Record	107%	Typical Rookie Race Lap time
Pontiac Solstice	58.733 (G.Huttu) *non Rookie car*	1:02.844	1:01 – 1:03
Spec Racer Ford	54.585 (P.Vasilopanagos)	58.406	0:58 – 1:00
Skip Barber F2000	53.865 (G.Huttu)	57.636	0:57 – 0:58
VW Jetta TDi	-	-	-

Charlotte Motor Speedway – Road Course

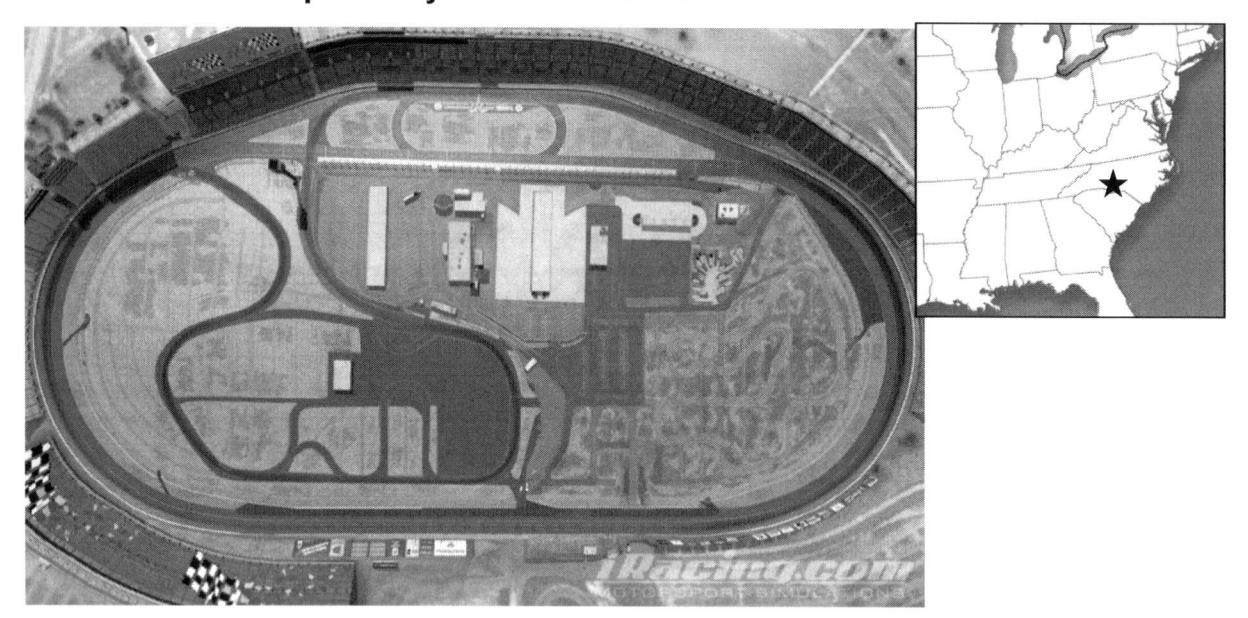

Description (From iRacing.com)

"Opened in 1960 by Bruton Smith and NASCAR driving legend Curtis Turner with the running of the longest stock car race in history, the World 600, a year later the 1.5-mile the Charlotte Motor Speedway was in bankruptcy, done in by a huge infield rock formation that ballooned construction costs far beyond what its two founders had forecast.

"Almost 50 years later nearly everything is different. More than 160,000 seats ring the race track, which was the first superspeedway to install lights for night racing; the first race track to incorporate a condominium apartment complex overlooking the racing surface; the first to build an office complex with the same view; and the first to open a year-round club where members can spectate during races and socialize with fellow club members at other times. Everything is very different from 1960 except for one thing; Charlotte Motor Speedway is still owned by Bruton Smith.

"Actually Charlotte Motor Speedway is today the queen of a six-track, publically-traded motorsports empire controlled by Smith. Ousted from the track in 1962, Smith went on a successful career in automotive retailing and by 1975 was able to buy back control. With the legendary H.A. "Humpy" Wheeler managing the day-to-day operations and promoting the races with flair and imagination, the track was soon among the most successful in the world.

"Today the Charlotte Motor Speedway complex incorporates not just the 1.5-mile quad oval with its 24-degree banking in the corners and 5-degree banked straightaways, but a 2.25-mile road course – that ancient rock formation provides sufficient elevation change to give one of the challenging infield corners a blind apex – and a quarter-mile asphalt oval utilizing part of the speedway's frontstretch and pit road (all three of which are included in the iRacing.com simulation).

"The facility also includes a 0.6 mile karting layout in the speedway's infield; a one-fifth-mile oval outside Turn Three of the superspeedway, and a state-of-the-art four-tenths-mile clay oval just across Highway 29. And soon construction will commence on a quarter-mile drag strip, scheduled to host professional drag racing. If it races on four wheels, there's a place for it to run at Charlotte Motor Speedway."

Charlotte Motor Speedway – Road Course: Driving Description

You will be carrying maximum speed as you cross the start/finish line and immediately after that you will need to brake hard and downshift and hit your turn in point. You may need to coast briefly until you can can be sure the car will not hit the wall on the right. If it is safe bring back the throttle and hold it through turn two. Just after straightening out the exit of turn two you will need to brake hard briefly for turn three.

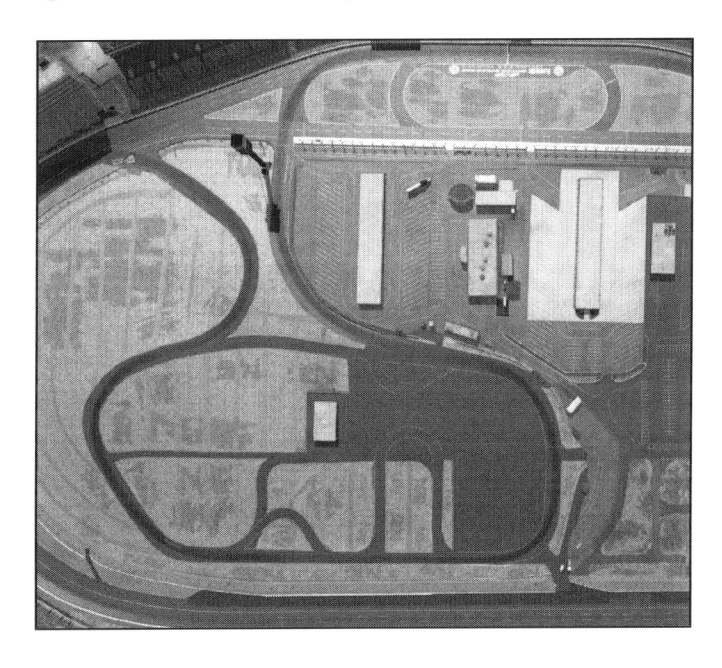

Turn three can be cut a little bit, but I find it is safest to hit the apex and swing out to the left at exit. Do not get back onto full throttle, although a little will be ok. You will very soon need to slow down further for turn four. Make sure you get enough speed bled away on entry since it is easy to over-do this corner. Messing up the exit because of a bad/aggressive entry will waste a lot of time in the grass and dirt.

The next turn requires lots of practice to take at high speed. I tend to brake more than most do here but in my races I have gained positions here from drivers taking higher risks with this turn. The loss of time by off-track mishaps in the infield section cannot be over-stated. A little tap of the brakes when setting up the entry is all it takes for a little insurance of getting this turn right every time.

Not long after straightening out the exit, you will need to brake hard and earlier than you think to tackle the tricky right hander. Many people spin here, so make certain you slow down enough to maintain control and then you can begin massaging the throttle pedal as you wind your way through the next two lefts leading onto the back straight. Do not be over aggressive in the first of the two lefts, since a slight touch of the grass will almost surely send you into the retaining wall. Be careful not to cut the second left too much as going too far over the patch of grass will result in an incident point. The rest of the lap is flat out. Keep the car down low through the turns but do not touch the flat (apron) as this will upset the car and cause you to lose control.

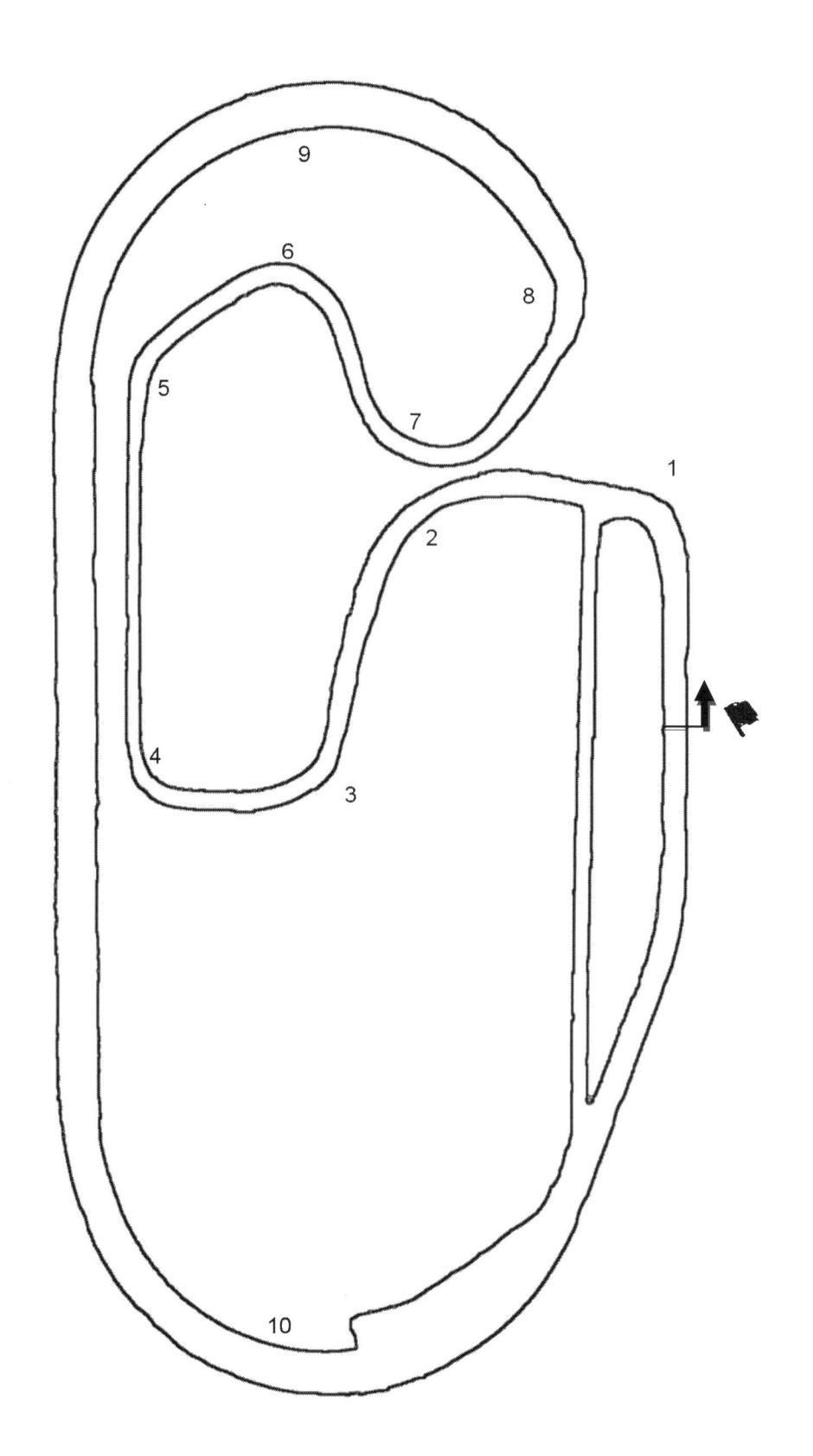

Charlotte Motor Speedway – Road Course: Vital Statistics

Track Name	Charlotte Motor Speedway (formerly known as "Lowes Motor Speedway")
Location	Concord, NC, USA
Website	http://www.charlottemotorspeedway.com/
Contact Names	Admin/SMI: (704) 455-3239 feedback@charlottemotorspeedway.com
Important Events	NASCAR (Cup, Nationwide, Trucks), Legends
Street Address	5555 Concord Parkway South, Concord, NC 28027
Mailing Address	PO Box 600, Concord, NC 28026
Phone	(704) 455-3200
Fax	(704) 455-4418 (Administration)
Time Zone	EST/EDT (GMT -0500/-0400)
Latitude, Longitude	35.350869° N, -80.683589° W
Altitude [m]	666 ft | 203 m
# Turns	12 (Road Course)
	12 (Infield Road Course)
	4 (Oval)
	4 (Legends Oval)
Distance	2.25 mi | 3.62 km (Road Course)
	0.72 mi | 1.16 km (Infield Road Course)
	1.5 mi | 2.41 km (Oval)
	0.25 mi | 0.40 km (Legends Oval)
Laps for Time Trial (TT)	6 (Road Course)
	10 (Infield Road Course)
	10 (Oval)
	10 (Legends Oval)

Track Element	Length; Minimum Radius [ft | m]
S/F Straight	1312 | 400
T1	213 | 65
T2	360 | 110
Straight	210 | 64
T3	250 | 76
T4	174 | 53
Straight	646 | 197
T5	344 | 105
Straight	141 | 43
T6	154 | 47
Straight	62 | 19
T7	220 | 67
T8	279 | 85
T9	685 | 209 (24° banking)
Back Straight	1673 | 510 (5° banking)
T10	625 | 190 (24° banking)

Car	iRacing World Record	107%	Typical Rookie Race Lap time
Pontiac Solstice (R)	1:25.525 (M.Dell'Orco)	1:31.512	1:28 – 1:32
Spec Racer Ford	1:20.375 (F.Hermann)	1:26.001	1:24 – 1:27
Skip Barber F2000	1:20.522 (D.Frattini)	1:26.159	1:23 – 1:26
VW Jetta TDi	-	-	-

Charlotte Motor Speedway – Infield Road Course

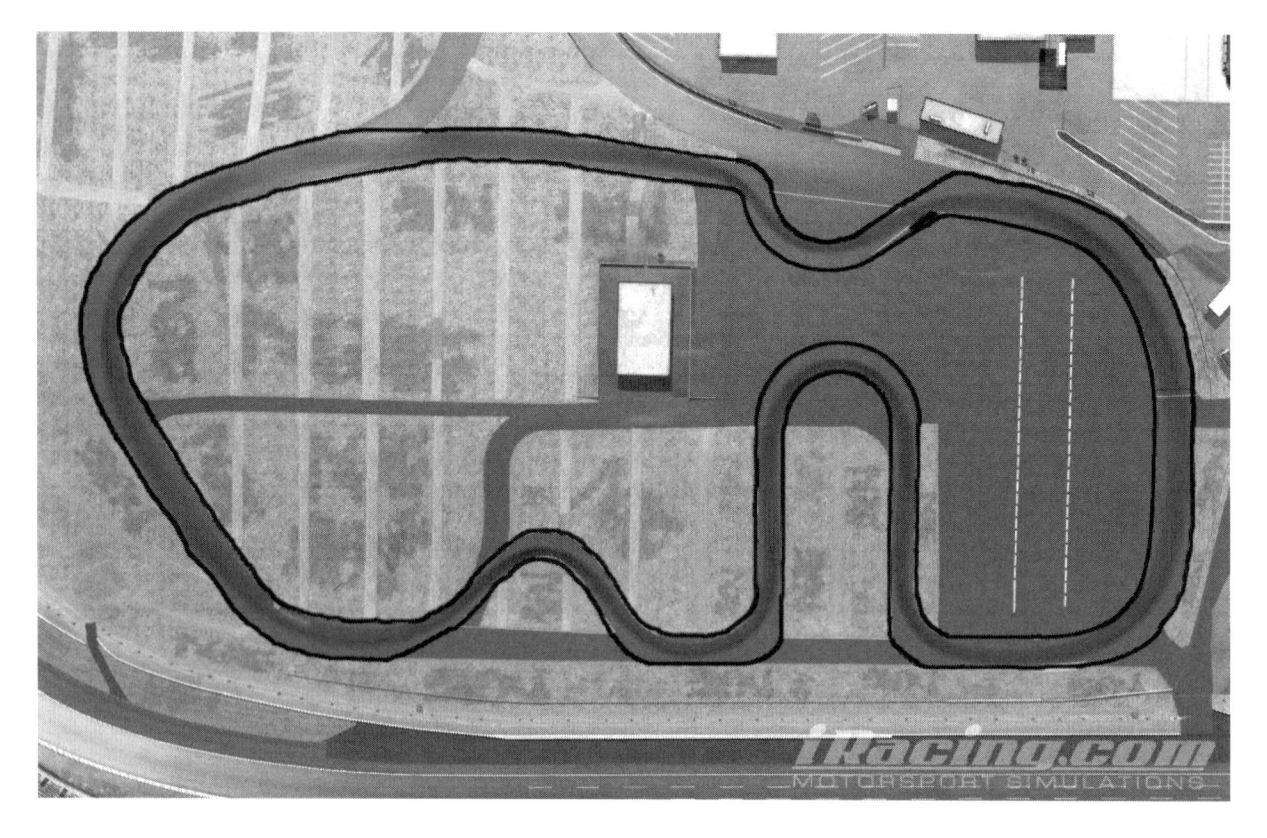

Charlotte Motor Speedway – Infield Road Course: Driving Description

This track will use mostly the low end of the transmission - first and second in the Skip Barber, with a brief time in third approaching the chicane with barrels. This is a good track to practice tight turns and to reinforce the old racing rule "slow in, fast out". Overdriving the tight turns of this track will always cost you time, but smooth driving and calm turn entry will allow you to get onto the power sooner.

The start/finish line can barely be called a straight, since you are always working the steering wheel. Coming into turn one balance the turn in with the pedals as much as the steering wheel before dropping it down first for entry to the tight turn two. Hold this gear through the next hairpin, then though the following double right plus left/right complex and roll back onto the throttle as you get onto the relatively open section following turn 6. However, this break doesn't last long as you'll need to get back onto the brakes to take the right hand crest which leads to the only relatively straight portion of the track. But beware of the bad dip and bump which can make the car unstable. I find this is a good place to do an off-throttle upshift to keep control of the car. But this higher gear will not be needed for long, as the chicane with the barrels comes up fast.

Hard on the brakes, but careful not to lock them, and straighten out the chicane as much as possible. Take care not to throw the car around or get too aggressive since the barrels will easily knock your wheels out of alignment and make continuing impossible. Once past the last barrel, you are already accelerating a little while turning onto the start/finish straight.

Tracks iRacing Paddock Page 99

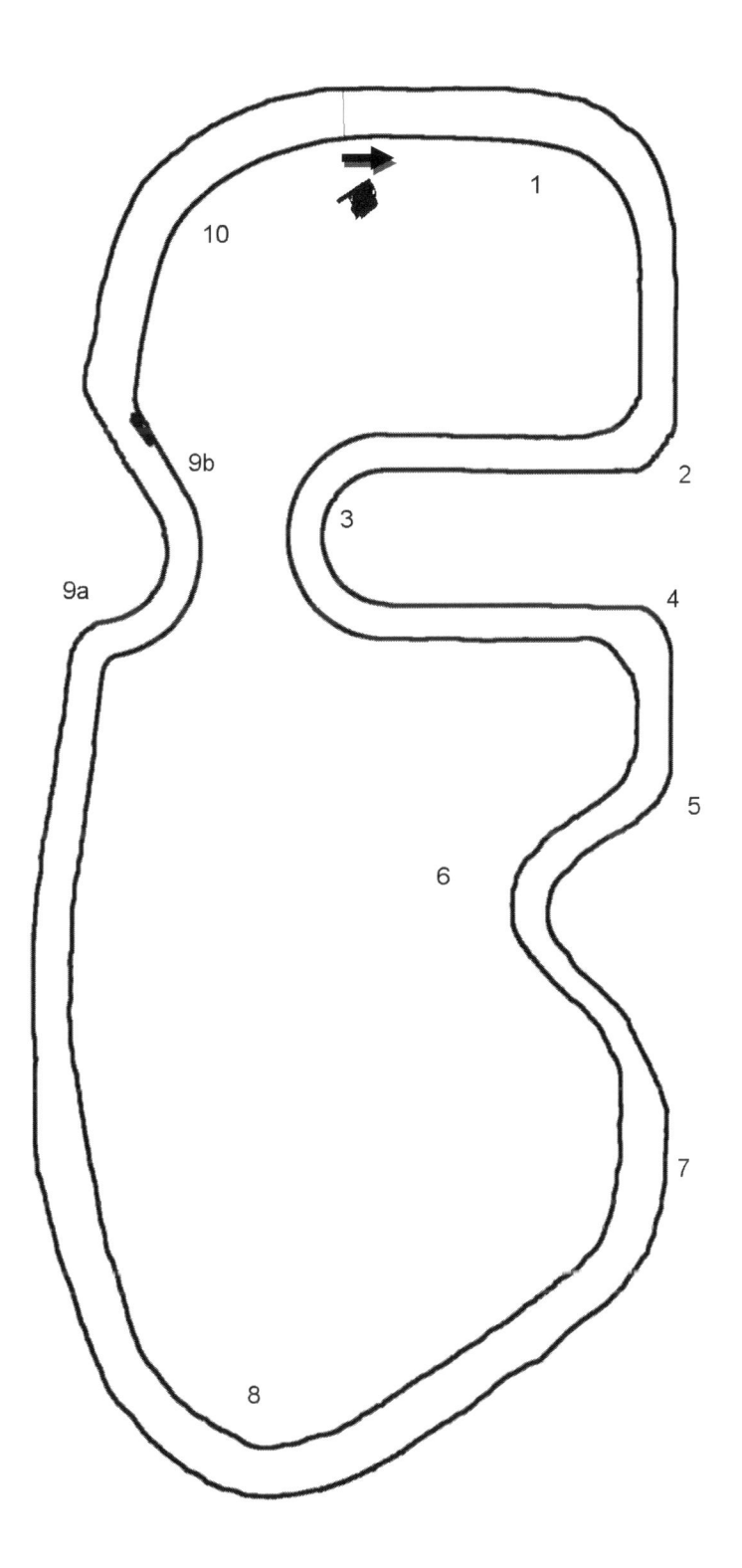

Centripetal Circuit

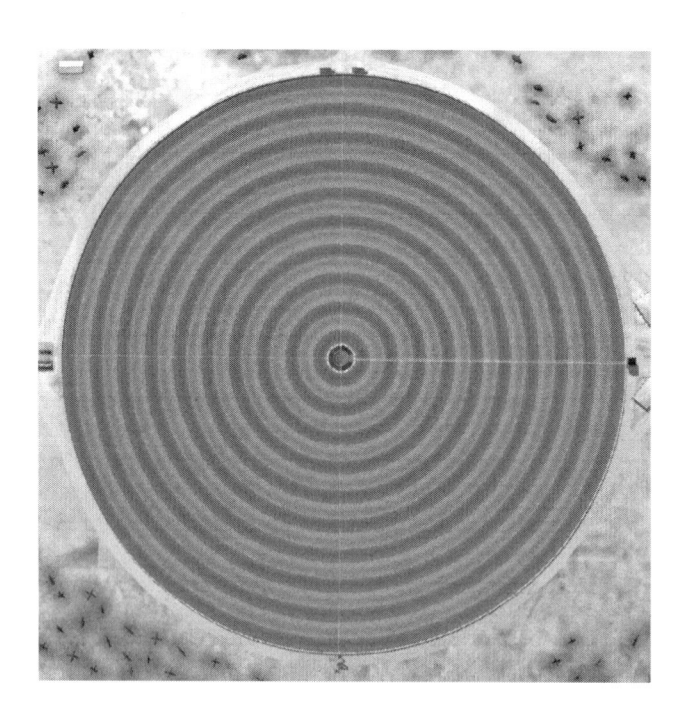

The iRacing skidpad track, known as Centripetal Circuit, is an excellent tool for beginners and experienced drivers alike to get a feel for the car and how it behaves approaching the limit of grip. The basic concept is to choose a radius to work with (I typically choose 50m to evaluate tighter turns and 150m to test fast turns) and then accelerate until you feel the car starting to lose the ability to maintain the turning radius, at which point you back off the throttle and thereafter balance the steering (with as little input as possible) and the throttle to maximize your speed while still holding to the chosen radius.

The average speed or lap time can be related back to the lateral acceleration by simple formulas according to the radius. But beyond simple curiosity about lap times and acceleration figures, this track can provide valuable lessons in being able to feel the grip in the tires and allow the driver to improve the ability to hold the car closer to the limit of grip without fear of losing control. This is one of the key skills a driver must learn and the centripetal circuit is the best tool to achieve it. I highly recommend occasionally spending time there to improve your cornering and car control skills.

FIRST Official Sporting Code – Version 2010.1.15.01

Note- this copy of the Sporting code is for casual reference only. Since the code is updated occasionally, only the current Sporting Code listed at members.iracing.com is considered the actual enforceable rules for the service.

1. General Principles

1.1. iRacing.com and FIRST

    1.1.1. iRacing.com exists to create the world's most authentic racing simulations, enable and organize real-time, online racing, and advance and expand motorsport.

    1.1.2. FIRST is the global sanctioning body for internet racing conducted through and by iRacing.com. Its mission is to organize, facilitate and execute internet racing competitions, providing structure, consistency and fairness.

    1.1.3. FIRST, as governed by its board of directors, shall be the sole sporting authority entitled to make and enforce regulations for internet racing competitions as hosted by iRacing.com.

    1.1.4. FIRST may from time to time elect to enter into co-sanctioning agreements or other similar partnerships with other motorsport sanctioning bodies, clubs or organizations to facilitate the organization and execution of a specific internet racing event or series of events.

1.2. FIRST Structure

    1.2.1. FIRST shall be governed by a Board of Directors, the chairman of which shall be appointed by iRacing.com Motorsport Simulations, LLC. Other directors shall be appointed by the chairman of FIRST.

    1.2.2. The FIRST Board of Directors shall establish the FIRST Competition Board to preside over all FIRST business related to matters of internet racing.

    1.2.3. The FIRST Competition Board may consist of voting and non-voting members and may, at the discretion of the Board of Directors, convene general meetings with both voting and non-voting members, as well as private meetings open only to voting members.

1.3. FIRST Sporting Code

    1.3.1. To ensure fair and consistent governance of internet racing competition, FIRST has established the FIRST Sporting Code.

    1.3.2. The FIRST Sporting Code, and any addenda, shall govern all internet racing events sanctioned by FIRST.

    1.3.3. It is the obligation and responsibility of all iRacing.com members to read, understand and abide by the FIRST Sporting Code.

    1.3.4. FIRST may from time to time, at its sole discretion, revise any or all of the FIRST Sporting Code.

    1.3.5. Substantive changes to the FIRST Sporting Code will be published as official notifications on http://members.iracing.com.

    1.3.6. FIRST may publish supplementary regulations pertaining to an individual series and/or event. These supplementary regulations are intended to augment the FIRST Sporting Code and/or modify certain elements of the Code to ensure fair and consistent competition in the particular series or event to which the supplementary regulations apply.

    1.3.7. Unless specifically noted in the supplementary regulations, all rules set forth in the FIRST Sporting Code will apply to every FIRST-sanctioned event.

1.3.8. The FIRST Sporting Code affords every iRacing member assessed a penalty or named as a party to protest the right to appeal a decision made by FIRST (See Appeals, Section 9 below). Upon final resolution of such appeals, however, application and interpretation of the FIRST Sporting Code by FIRST officials shall be final and binding.

1.4. Conduct

1.4.1. Principles

1.4.1.1. At iRacing we believe that racing in the virtual world is as much a form of motorsport as racing in the physical one. Our expectation is that all members of our community – racers, officials and employees – will conduct themselves in the same way as a race participant would at an event in the physical world. Each of us owes every other member of the iRacing community the same courtesy and respect that we expect to receive ourselves.

1.4.1.2. Much of the satisfaction of being a member of our community comes from the personal relationships that are formed and maintained here. For that reason, we require members to register using their real names, which, in addition to facilitating friendships, promotes personal responsibility.

1.4.1.3. Emotions will run as high in our races as they do in all competitive environments. But rude behavior – whether in actions behind the wheel, in oral communications through in-sim chat, or in writing on forums – damages social relationships and has no place here.

1.4.1.4. The Terms of Use and End User Licensing Agreement to which you agreed upon joining iRacing stipulates that iRacing – including its sanctioning organization FIRST – will be the judge of what constitutes inappropriate on-track or interpersonal behavior, and shall have the authority to impose penalties up to and including revocation of membership. We will have zero tolerance for deliberate bad behavior, whether on- or off-track. Those individuals who are habitually unable to treat others in an appropriate fashion will find themselves on the outside looking in.

1.4.2. On-Track Conduct

1.4.2.1. iRacing places a high value on responsible driving and fair competition. Accidents in racing are inevitable; they are a natural consequence of close competition. But the FIRST graduated licensing program stresses the development of driving skills and the avoidance of accidents, rewarding safe driving and minimizing the number of on-track accidents.

1.4.2.2. In the physical world, the risk of injury and expensive car repairs serves as a natural deterrent to reckless driving. Because those risks don't exist in the virtual world, iRacing has developed a system that automatically calculates a driver's safety record through each lap in every official on-track session. The system does not assess blame for an incident, so responsibility for avoiding crashes still resides with each individual driver.

1.4.2.3. While it is not feasible for iRacing to directly monitor every on-track session, FIRST officials will randomly select sessions to monitor. Drivers can also report reckless and/or erratic driving and attempts at on-track intimidation (See Reckless Driving, sections 5.1.11 and 5.2.11, below) to FIRST officials by emailing a complete description of the incident (including series name, session time, and drivers involved in the incident) to Protest@iRacing.com (See Protests, Section 8, below). Failure to drive with respect for other competitors will lead to substantial sanctions. Those who habitually engage in bad on-track behavior will be removed from our community.

1.4.3. Voice and Text Chat

1.4.3.1. iRacing provides means for racers to communicate with one another before, during and after on-track sessions. The high emotions that are a normal part of close racing do not justify verbally abusive or other inappropriate expressions toward officials or other racers. Disrespectful communications, including foul or threatening language and insults, will not be tolerated and will lead to the cancellation of the offender's membership.

1.4.4. Forums and iRacing World

1.4.4.1. The iRacing forums and iRacing World are the social backbone of our community, providing a way for members to interact with one another, exchange information and build friendships. Disagreements are part of the landscape, but in order to maintain a pleasant environment for all community members, participants must not use rude or hostile language. Posts that attempt to publicly confront, accuse or attack another member or official are forbidden. Those who engage in a pattern of such behavior will face penalties that may include revocation of membership.

1.4.4.2. The Private Messaging function is considered part of the iRacing Forums and iRacing World, and as such, the same standards for conduct apply to all private messages. Foul or threatening language and insults will not be tolerated and will lead to the cancellation of the offender's membership.

2. FIRST Licenses

2.1. Principles

2.1.1. In an effort to provide the best possible racing experience for all competitors, iRacing.com™ has instituted a licensing process for all members.

2.1.2. Members start at Rookie and progress. Higher-level licenses are awarded based on on-track safety record and experience. Each racing series is restricted to certain license levels, grouping drivers with similar safety records. iRatings, which measure driver skills based on competitive results, do not impact FIRST licenses.

2.1.3. FIRST licenses are awarded (or lost) during the season and at the completion of iRacing.com™ Season. Members earn licenses sequentially within a particular iRacing.com™ Category, Road Racing or Oval Track Racing. (See Section 2.8)

2.2. Earning a FIRST License

2.2.1. Each new iRacing.com™ member starts with a Rookie License for each racing Category, Road and Oval. Thereafter, FIRST licenses must be earned.

2.2.2. License advancement is based on two factors:

2.2.3. Completion of a minimum participation requirement.

2.2.4. Achievement of a minimum safety record.

2.2.5. Licenses can be earned or lost during the season as well as upon the completion of a season. (See Section 2.8)

2.2.6. Licenses must be obtained in sequential order, and although a member's safety record in one racing Category does have some influence on his or her safety record in another racing Category, the minimum requirements and license progression are Category-specific.

2.3. License Levels

2.3.1. Rookie License (including Rookie and Advanced Rookie) – Indicated by Red Stripe on Car and License

2.3.2. Class D FIRST License – indicated by Orange Stripe on Car and License

2.3.3. Class C FIRST License – indicated by Yellow Stripe on Car and License

2.3.4. Class B FIRST License – indicated by Green Stripe on Car and License

2.3.5. Class A FIRST License – indicated by Blue Stripe on Car and License

2.3.6. iRacing.com™ Pro Series License (limited to the top rated drivers in the world) – indicated by Black Stripe on Car and License

2.4. Minimum Participation Requirements (MPR)

2.4.1. Rookies are required to participate in at least four official Time Trial sessions OR two official Race Sessions during the current 12-week racing season in order to earn a Class D license (provided their safety record meets the minimum standard) in a particular category.

2.4.2. All non-rookies are required to participate in at least four official Time Trial sessions OR four official Race sessions during the current 12-week racing season in the series in which they are licensed in order to be promoted (provided their safety record meets the minimum standard) in a particular category.

2.4.3. For a race to be official, the race must meet the official minimum field size requirements. For a driver to be credited with an official race start, the driver must complete at least one lap in an official race session and receive championship points.

2.4.4. A Time Trial is only official if a driver completes the required number of consecutive incident free laps and receives a Fastest "X" Lap Avg. time in the session.

2.4.5. Drivers must participate in a series with minimum license eligibility requirements that match the driver's current license level in a given category. Sessions in a series with minimum license eligibility requirements below the driver's current license level (see section 2.9.3, "racing down") will not count.

Example: a driver with a Class D road racing license may complete the minimum participation requirements for the current season by competing in four Time Trials or four Race sessions in the Class D Skip Barber Race Series. But if the same driver runs sessions in the Advanced Rookie Solstice series (racing down), the sessions will not count towards his/her minimum participation requirement.

2.5. Incidents

2.5.1. The iRacing.com software monitors all official on-track sessions (not including Testing) and any incidents that occur therein. Each incident type is given a certain value (see list below), and the software automatically tallies each driver's incidents for each session. (See Table 2.5)

Table 2.5

Light contact with another driver	0x
wheels off the racing surface	1x
Loss of control	2x
Contact with other objects	2x
Heavy contact with another driver	4x

2.5.2. Non-additive nature of incidents – In the event of multiple concurrent incidents, only the most serious (e.g., 4x vs. 1x) is counted.

2.5.3. The iRacing.com™ software does not attempt to determine fault. Incidents are assessed to all involved drivers individually on a no-fault basis – no matter the circumstances.

2.6. Safety Rating

2.6.1. Safety Rating is a measure of a driver's overall safety record and is calculated using a formula that takes into account the number of corners a driver passes through and the number and severity of incidents that driver accumulates in the process. These factors are averaged over a set number of laps and updated as each new session is finished.

2.6.2. Each class of license (in each category, Oval or Road) has a related range of Safety Ratings: 0.00 – 4.99.

2.7. Corner & Incident Multipliers

2.7.1. iRacing.com™ places a high priority on safe driving at all times, but races, and other sessions when incidents can directly affect more than one competitor, are more important than Time Trials and single-car Qualifying. Accordingly, Corner & Incident Multipliers are applied when averaging a recent session into a driver's Safety Rating.

2.7.2. Current Corner & Incident Multipliers are shown below in Table 2.7. Note that incidents are counted throughout each session, including during the cool-down period after the checkered flag has been shown.

Table 2.7

Session Type	Sim Session	Weight
Practice	Lone Practice	0.0
Practice	Open Practice	0.0
Qualify	Lone Qualifying (Oval)	0.35
Qualify	Open Qualifying (Road)	0.5
Time Trial	Time Trial	0.35
Race	Warm Up	0.5
Race	Race	1
Unofficial Race	Warm Up	0.35
Unofficial Race	Race	0.35

2.8. Minimum Safety Requirements

2.8.1. A driver must achieve and maintain a Safety Rating within a certain range to advance to the next license level. A driver can track his or her safety record by the Safety Rating number on each category-specific license.

2.8.2. Drivers will start out with a Rookie License with a Safety Rating of 2.50 in each category. As they complete sessions safely, their Safety Rating will rise. Conversely, multiple incidents will cause their safety rating to fall.

2.8.3. Promotion

2.8.3.1. Fast Track: Drivers having earned a 4.00 Safety Rating at any point during the season and having met the MPR will be promoted to the next higher license level.

2.8.3.2. End of Season: Drivers having earned a 3.00 Safety Rating during the course of a season will be promoted to the next higher license level at the conclusion of that season (provided the minimum participation requirement is met).

2.8.4. Demotion

2.8.4.1. During the Season: Drivers whose safety ratings drop below 1.0 at any point during a season, including participants in the Pro Series, will be demoted to a lower license level.

2.8.4.1.1. Pro-License holders will have to improve their A level license to a 4.0 safety rating and only then will be automatically reinstated." Moreover, if they drop below an A level license, they will have to meet the requirements to work their way back up to an A level and the 4.0 safety rating.

2.8.4.2. Rookie and Class D License holders are not subject to in-season or end-of-season demotions.

2.8.4.3. Class A drivers are subject to only demotions during the season unless said driver was demoted from a Pro-License.

2.8.4.4. End of Season: Drivers with a 2.00 - 2.99 Safety Rating will remain at the same license level, and drivers with a Safety Rating below 2.00 will be demoted to the next-lower license level at the conclusion of the season.

2.9. Series Eligibility

2.9.1. In order to be eligible to compete in a given iRacing.com™ racing series, a driver must possess a category-specific license meeting the minimum series eligibility requirement.

2.9.2. In all cases, drivers may "race down," participating in series primarily intended for drivers at lower license levels.

2.9.3. Rookie Series are open to all iRacing members, rookie competition license or higher.

2.9.4. Advanced Rookie Series are open to Rookie license holders who have achieved a Safety Rating of 3.00 or higher and to drivers holding a Class D or above license.

2.9.5. Class D Series are open to drivers holding a Class D, Rookie License holders with a 4.00 Safety Rating who've not yet completed the MPR for promotion, and all licenses above D..

2.9.6. Class C Series are open to drivers holding Class C, D License holders with a 4.00 Safety Rating who've not yet completed the MPR for promotion, and all licenses above C.

2.9.7. Class B Series are open to drivers holding Class B, C License holders with a 4.00 Safety Rating who've not yet completed the MPR for promotion, and all licenses above B.

2.9.8. Class A Series are open to drivers holding Class A, B License holders with a 4.00 Safety Rating who've not yet completed the MPR for promotion, and Pro-License holders

2.9.9. iRacing.com™ Pro Series are open only to the top Pro License holders for a specific category.

2.10. Vehicle Classes

2.10.1. FIRST classifies all competition vehicles based on weight-to-power ratio and other factors. There are six classes of vehicles: Rookie, Advanced Rookie, Class D, Class C, Class B and Class A.

3. Driver Skill Ratings

3.1. iRating

3.1.1. iRatings are a measure of racing proficiency and exist to ensure competitive racing and championships by maximizing the chances that similarly skilled drivers compete against one another.

3.1.2. iRatings are the primary factor in assigning drivers to Divisions for the series in which they compete, maximizing competition and allowing members to advance to higher, more prestigious Driver Divisions as their skills improve or return to a lower Division if the competition proves too difficult. (See Section 4.5, Divisions)

3.1.3. iRatings are used to gauge the level of difficulty of a given race, influencing the calculation of championship points to be awarded for each finishing position based on the strength of the field. The higher the degree of difficulty, the more points are available to each driver in the race. (See Section 4.7.2.1, Strength of Field)

3.1.4. Every driver shall have a separate iRating for each category (Oval and Road). Each category-specific iRating is automatically calculated and updated to reflect the driver's performance in any races joined in that category.

3.1.5. Only races in a given category affect a driver's iRating in that category. There is no cross-category influence on iRating.

3.1.6. Drivers gain iRating points by taking them away from other drivers in Official Race Sessions. (See Section 5.2.2.1, Field Sizes Per Race)

3.1.7. iRatings are not visible to members holding Rookie Licenses.

3.2. ttRating (Time Trial Rating)

3.2.1. ttRatings are a measure of proficiency in the Time Trial discipline and compare an individual driver's best average lap time at a particular track against the best recorded average lap time for the same car at that track.

3.2.2. ttRatings are the primary factor in assigning drivers to Divisions for the series in which they compete, maximizing competition and allowing members to advance to higher and more prestigious Driver Divisions as their skills improve or return to a lower Division if the competition proves too difficult. (See Section 4.5, Divisions)

3.2.3. Each driver shall have a separate ttRating for each category (Oval and Road). Each category-specific ttRating is automatically calculated and updated to reflect the driver's performance in any Time Trial sessions joined in that category.

3.2.4. Only Time Trial sessions in a given category affect a driver's ttRating in that category. There is no cross-category influence on ttRating.

3.2.5. Drivers gain ttRating points by improving their time trial relative to the best time trial on record for the same car at a given track.

3.2.6. A driver's track ttRating is the average of his/her last 4 time trials at a given track.

3.2.7. ttRatings are calculated by averaging a driver's track ttRating at the last 8 tracks where he/she has completed an official time trial.

3.2.8. Drivers will not gain ttRating points by finishing ahead of drivers with a higher ttRating, nor lose points based other ttRatings. As a driver's average time trial for a given track gets closer to the existing record, he/she may gain ttRating points, if it moves further from the time trial record, he/she may lose ttRating points.

3.2.9. ttRatings are not visible to members holding Rookie Licenses.

4. Competition

4.1. Membership

4.1.1. Membership Status

4.1.1.1. An iRacing.com member is not an agent, servant or employee of iRacing.com or FIRST by virtue of such membership. With respect to any iRacing.com or FIRST related activities in which a Member engages, unless the Member is also an employee of FIRST or iRacing.com Motorsport Simulations, the Member shall act as and be deemed to be either an independent contractor or an employee of a person or entity other than iRacing.com or FIRST, and not an agent, servant or employee of iRacing.com or FIRST.

4.1.1.2. Each such Member assumes all responsibility, either by himself or his or her employer, for any charges, record keeping, premiums and taxes, if any, payable on any funds the Member may receive as a result of any activities as an iRacing.com Member and FIRST participant, including but not limited to, social security taxes, unemployment insurance taxes, workers compensation insurance, income taxes and withholding taxes.

4.1.1.3. Unless an exception is specifically granted by the FIRST Competition Board in writing in the form of supplementary series or event regulations, employees of iRacing.com or FIRST are ineligible for all competition awards and prizes.

4.1.2. Suspension

4.1.2.1. iRacing.com or FIRST may suspend a Member for a definite or indefinite period of time in the interest of internet racing, iRacing.com, FIRST or the membership. The affected Member may appeal such a suspension to the FIRST Competition Board.

4.1.3. Involuntary Termination

4.1.3.1. iRacing.com or FIRST may terminate a membership at any time in the interest of internet racing, iRacing.com, FIRST or the membership. Such Member shall have no right to receive, and neither iRacing.com nor FIRST shall be obligated to refund any part or all of the fees previously paid by the Member to iRacing.com. The affected Member may appeal such a termination to the FIRST Competition Board according to the procedure and subject to the limitations set forth in Section 9 of this document (Appeals).

4.1.4. Membership Required

4.1.4.1. Every person or entity who desires to participate in an Event as a driver must possess a current iRacing.com Membership authorizing participation in that capacity.

4.1.5. Membership Non-Transferable

4.1.5.1. An iRacing.com membership is non-transferable and non-assignable. It may be used only by the person or entity to which it is issued.

4.1.5.2. Running official sessions under another member's account is forbidden, as is supplying another member with personal account information (Username/Password) to enable him/her to run official sessions on an account other than his/her own. Either action will result in the account suspension of both the account holder and the person competing on his/her behalf. Neither driver will be eligible for premier series, such as the Pro-Series or Drivers World Championship Series, for a period of no less than one year.

4.1.6. Removal from an event

4.1.6.1. A FIRST Official may remove a member from an event to promote the orderly conduct of the Event. Sanctions issued during an event are not appealable.

4.2. Sanctioning

4.2.1. Event Sanctioning

4.2.1.1. A FIRST-sanctioned Event is an Event which awards championship points for Individual or Club Championships.

4.2.1.2. Individuals holding a current, valid FIRST Competition License for a Class of Vehicle are authorized to participate in Events within that Competition Class.

4.2.1.3. FIRST shall sanction two types of championships: INDIVIDUAL and CLUB.

4.2.2. Competition Calendar

4.2.2.1. FIRST shall publish an annual Competition Calendar on or before January 1st of each calendar year, dividing the year into four 12-week seasons.

4.2.2.2. Each season shall be subdivided into 12 individual race weeks.

4.2.3. Categories

4.2.3.1. FIRST-sanctioned competition is currently divided into two categories, based on the nature of the racing venue: ROAD and OVAL.

4.2.3.2. Although all elements of competition, including licenses, series, sessions, points and championships, are generally unique to a particular category, FIRST reserves the right to introduce competitions that include both ROAD and OVAL courses.

4.2.4. Series

4.2.4.1. Within each category, FIRST sanctions various racing series. Each series is defined by its season schedule (ordered list of host venues, including track configurations), vehicle and license eligibility requirements. FIRST reserves the right to modify any series schedule at any time. Any series schedule modifications will be published as official notifications on http://members.iracing.com.

4.2.4.2. FIRST sanctions two varieties of series: STANDARD and NON-STANDARD.

4.2.4.3. Standard series feature 12 weeks of competition at a defined list of venues for a defined range of license holders in a particular class of vehicles.

4.2.4.4. Non-standard series include four-week Rookie series and any other series that do not follow the normal 12-week season as set forth in the FIRST Competition Calendar.

4.2.4.5. FIRST may publish series-specific Supplemental Regulations for all non-standard series.

4.2.4.6. Within each standard series are two different driving competitions: RACE and TIME TRIAL. Members may compete in one or both.

4.2.5. Rookie Series

4.2.5.1. Rookie Series are non-standard series in both categories (Oval and Road) reserved for new iRacing.com members holding Rookie competition licenses. Rookie series are intended to be educational, allowing new members the opportunity to build skills, acclimate to the iRacing simulation software and community and the sport of internet racing.

4.2.5.2. Rookie series shall typically include four race weeks.

4.3. Competitor Releases

4.3.1. Advertising and Promotion Releases

4.3.1.1. Each member, by participating in any FIRST-sanctioned event, grants to iRacing.com, its authorized agents and assigns, an exclusive license to use and sublicense his or her name, likeness and performance, including photographs, images and sounds of such competitor and/or any vehicle that competitor drives in the event, in any way, medium or material (including but not limited to broadcasts by and through television, cable television, radio, pay-per-view, closed circuit television, satellite signal, digital signal, film productions, audiotape productions, transmissions over the Internet, public or private online services authorized by iRacing.com, sales and other commercial projects, and the like) for promoting, advertising and broadcasting, recording or reporting any FIRST-sanctioned event before, during and after such event, and each competitor hereby relinquishes to iRacing.com exclusively and in perpetuity all rights thereto for such purposes.

4.3.2. Broadcast and Other Rights

4.3.2.1. Each member, by participating in any FIRST-sanctioned event, acknowledges that iRacing.com, and its licenses and assigns, exclusively and in perpetuity owns any and all rights to broadcast, transmit, film, tape, capture, overhear, photograph, collect or record by any means, process, medium or device (including but not limited to broadcasts by and through television, cable television, radio, pay-per-view, closed circuit television, satellite signal, digital signal, film productions, audiotape productions, transmissions over the Internet, public or private online services authorized by iRacing.com, sales and other commercial projects, and the like), whether or not currently in existence, all images, sounds and data (including but not limited to in-car audio, in-car video, in-car radio, voice chat, text chat, other electronic transmissions between cars and crews, and timing and scoring information) arising from or during any FIRST-sanctioned event or the competitor's performance in the event, and that iRacing.com is and shall be the sole owner of any and all copyrights, intellectual property rights, and proprietary rights worldwide in and to these works and in and to any other works, copyrightable or otherwise, created from the images, sounds and data arising from or during any FIRST-sanctioned event and the competitor's performance in the event. Each competitor agrees to take all steps reasonably necessary, and all steps requested by iRacing.com, to protect, perfect or effectuate iRacing.com's ownership of other interest in these rights. Each competitor agrees not to take any action, nor cause others to take any action, nor enter into any third-party agreement which would contravene, diminish, encroach or infringe upon these iRacing.com rights.

4.4. Divisions

4.4.1. Racing

4.4.1.1. Each standard Race series will be divided into 10 competition divisions, grouping drivers of similar skill level in competition for the remainder of the season. Any standard series open to holders of rookie competition licenses shall include an eleventh division for any rookie license holders participating in that series.

4.4.1.2. At the beginning of the third race week of each season, the iRacing.com system will automatically partition each series into 10 (or 11 when appropriate) competition divisions based on the number of drivers who have competed in that series during the first two race weeks and the range of their current iRatings.

4.4.1.3. Drivers will be assigned to divisions based on their current iRating.

4.4.1.4. Drivers who have not participated in any official sessions during the first two weeks of the season will not be assigned to a division until they have participated in an official session.

4.4.1.5. Non-standard series (e.g., four-week rookie series) will not be segmented into divisions, unless otherwise stated in series-specific supplemental regulations.

4.4.2. Time Trial

4.4.2.1. Each standard Time Trial series will be divided into 10 competition divisions, grouping drivers of similar skill level in competition for the remainder of the season. Any standard series open to holders of rookie competition licenses shall include an eleventh division for any rookie license holders participating in that series.

4.4.2.2. At the beginning of the third race week of each season, the iRacing.com system will automatically partition each series into 10 (or 11 when appropriate) competition divisions based on the number of drivers who have competed in that series during the first two race weeks and the range of their current ttRatings.

4.4.2.3. Drivers will be assigned to divisions based on their current ttRating.

4.4.2.4. Drivers who have not participated in any official sessions during the first two weeks of the season will not be assigned to a division until they have participated in an official session

4.4.2.5. Non-standard series (e.g., four-week rookie series) will not be segmented into divisions, unless otherwise stated in series-specific supplemental regulations.

4.5. Sessions

4.5.1. Principle

4.5.1.1. Standard FIRST-sanctioned series include four types of official sessions: PRACTICE, QUALIFY, RACE and TIME TRIAL. Each session is subject to the same category, schedule, license and vehicle eligibility requirements, as well as all series- and event-specific supplemental regulations, as the series with which they are associated. EVENT points are scored in Official Series Races.

4.5.2. Testing

4.5.2.1. TESTING is unofficial and not associated with any particular series, season or category.

4.5.3. Practice

4.5.3.1. Practice sessions are unstructured practice time. Official lap times and incidents are recorded, but practice incidents are not factored into a driver's official safety rating calculation (see Licenses, sections 2.5 – 2.7 above)

4.5.3.2. Practice sessions are generally 30 minutes in length.

4.5.4. Qualifying

4.5.4.1. Qualifying sessions determine the overall weekly qualifying order, which is used to grid cars in race sessions. The order is updated throughout the week, and race sessions are gridded according to the qualifying order as it exists at the session start time.

4.5.4.2. Official lap times and incidents are recorded and factored into a driver's official safety rating calculation (see Licenses, sections 2.5 – 2.7 above).

4.5.4.3. Drivers who have not participated in at least one qualifying session during a given race week will start race sessions from the back of the grid. If there are multiple drivers without qualifying times in a given race session, they will be gridded behind all drivers who have posted times, from highest iRating to lowest.

4.5.4.4. Road racing qualifying sessions are generally 30 minutes in length and can include multiple cars on track at once.

4.5.4.5. Oval-category series feature single-car qualifying, with a driver's qualifying time being the best of four laps.

4.5.5. Time Trial

4.5.5.1. Time Trials are single-car sessions in which a driver must complete a prescribed number of consecutive laps as quickly as possible and without incident. The best average lap time through a completed sequence is recorded as the driver's Time Trial time. Any incident invalidates the current sequence.

4.5.5.2. The number of laps in a full sequence will vary from track to track and configuration to configuration and will be indicated in the Series-specific supplemental regulations.

4.5.5.3. If a driver completes more than the prescribed number of consecutive, incident-free laps, the system will automatically record the average lap time through best sequence of consecutive laps.

4.5.5.4. Official lap times and incidents are recorded and factored into a driver's official safety rating calculation (see Licenses, sections 2.5 – 2.7 above).

4.5.6. Race

4.5.6.1. Race sessions are real-time competition with multiple cars on track at the same time.

4.5.6.2. Official lap times and incidents are recorded and factored into a driver's official safety rating calculation (see Licenses, sections 2.5 – 2.7 above).

4.5.6.3. All Official Race sessions are recorded and factored into a driver's official iRating calculation (see iRatings, section 3.1 above).

4.6. Individual Points

4.6.1. Race Points

4.6.1.1. RACE EVENT points are scored in Official Series Races.

4.6.1.2. Races are valued by the Strength of Field (SOF), which is based on the iRatings of the drivers in the field. The higher the average strength of field, the more points are available for each finishing position.

4.6.1.3. Race event points are adjusted for field size. The larger the field the smaller the difference in points awarded for each finishing position.

4.6.1.4. RACE WEEK POINTS: Drivers may compete in as many Official Series Races as they choose in a given race week.

4.6.1.5. The best 50% of a driver's race performances (based on points scored) in a given Race Week will be averaged at the conclusion of each Official Series Race during the week. The final average at the conclusion of the Race Week will be the driver's Race Week Point Total and count towards the season championships in that series.

4.6.1.5.1. Example: If a driver competes in five official races in the Skip Barber Series in a given week, the driver's best three race-point totals are averaged and those points go towards the driver's season championship points total.

4.6.1.6. SEASON RACE POINTS are calculated by totaling the race week points earned by a driver in a given series in a single season. A driver's best 8 weeks of the 12 Race weeks will count towards Individual and Club Championships.

4.6.2. Time Trial Points

4.6.2.1. Time Trial points are scored in Time Trial Sessions. A driver's best average lap time over the prescribed sequence of laps is recorded and points awarded.

4.6.2.2. Time Trial points are awarded linearly. There is no strength of field calculated. The driver with the fastest average lap time over the prescribed sequence of laps is awarded 100 points. All drivers below are awarded points linearly with a precision of 1/1000th of a point between positions.

4.6.2.3. Time Trial points are kept in real time until the end of a Race Week, when they are frozen and finalized.

4.6.2.4. SEASON TIME TRIAL POINTS are calculated by totaling a driver's weekly Time Trial points, as finalized at the conclusion of each race week. A driver's best 8 weeks of the 12-race-week season will count towards the Overall and Divisional Time Trial Championships.

4.7. Club Points

4.7.1. Points are calculated such that a driver earns 1 point for every competitor who finishes behind him and loses 1 Club point for every driver who finishes ahead of him in an officially-sanctioned race. (See Annex A)

4.7.2. A driver with a Club Score for the race of less than zero receives zero Club Points. Club Standings will be based on total Club Points.

4.7.3. A multiplier is used to balance the size of clubs. Such multiplier is based on the number of paid subscribers a club has at the beginning of each racing year. The multiplier will be reset at the end of each racing year at a minimum or more often as determined by iRacing.

4.7.4. The multiplier shall be a proportion of the club with the most current paid subscribers. Example:

4.7.5. Example: If the largest current paid subscriber club is California with 500 subscribers, then: Club Subscribers Multiplier California 500 1.000 Ohio 250 2.000 Georgia 300 1.666 Atlantic 120 4.166

4.7.6. All License classes including Rookie can score Club Points. Every series is active for Club Scoring except Rookie, Pro, and Drivers World Championship Series; however Advanced Rookies Series is eligible for Club points.

4.7.7. Club points are updated in real time throughout the season and fluctuate until the end of the season.

4.7.8. Divisions are no longer a factor in club scoring.

4.8. Individual Championships

4.8.1. iRacing.com World Championships

4.8.1.1. The individual race championships shall be known as the iRacing.com World Championships and will be decided by a driver's accumulation of points in official RACE sessions in a given season.

4.8.1.2. Individual championship competition involves a single driver competing for a season title by accumulating race week points in official sessions.

4.8.1.3. Drivers may participate in as many official sessions as they like during a given race week. Points will be finalized at the end of the race week and recorded as the driver's official points for that week. These finalized race week points count towards a driver's season-ending point total.

4.8.1.4. Each standard series shall crown an overall season race champion and divisional race champions for each of 10 competition divisions.

4.8.1.5. Standard series open to rookie competition license holders will crown champions for 11 competition divisions, including the 10 regular divisions and the eleventh rookie-only division. (See Divisions, section 4.4.1 above).

4.8.1.6. Although Race Points, Race Week Points and Season Race Points are calculated, non-standard, four-week Rookie Series do not include seasonal championships.

4.8.2. Time Trial World Championships

4.8.2.1. The individual Time Trial championships shall be known as the iRacing.com World Championship Time Trials and will be decided by a driver's accumulation of points in TIME TRIAL sessions in a given season.

4.8.2.2. Each standard series shall crown an overall season Time Trial champion and divisional Time Trial champions for each of 10 competition divisions (see Divisions, section 4.4.2 above).

4.8.2.3. Standard series open to rookie competition license holders will crown champions for 11 competition divisions, including the 10 regular divisions and the eleventh rookie-only division. (See Divisions, section 4.4.2 above).

4.8.2.4. Although Time Trial Points, Race Week Time Trial Points and Season Time Trial Points are calculated, non-standard, four-week Rookie series do not include seasonal championships.

4.9. Club Championships

4.9.1. Club championships shall be known as the World Cup of iRacing. (See Annex A)

4.9.2. Club championships are contests between geographically-based clubs competing for season titles and shall be decided by aggregating the Individual Championship point totals from eligible drivers (See Club Points, section 4.7 above) within the club across all series and divisions.

5. Race Procedures

5.1. Road Course

5.1.1. Registration

5.1.1.1. All FIRST Sanctioned races are available for registration 30 Minutes prior to the start of the event.

5.1.1.2. A timer will be visible in the Member Website Race Panel counting down to the start of the Race Session.

5.1.1.3. Anytime between the opening of registration and 2 minutes prior to the session start time, drivers may withdraw from the Race Session without a point or iRating penalty.

5.1.1.4. Withdrawing from a Race Session with 2 minutes or fewer left on the countdown timer may result in a forfeit.

5.1.1.5. Any driver forfeiting a race will be credited with a last-place finish and earn 0 points for that race. The race will be counted in the driver's Race Week Average (see RACE WEEK POINTS, section 4.6.1.4 above)

5.1.1.6. Any Driver forfeiting a race will be credited with a last-place finish and his/her iRating will reflect a negative change equal to a last place finish.

5.1.2. Race Splits

5.1.2.1. FIRST and iRacing.com seek to have similarly skilled drivers racing together in each event.

5.1.2.2. Should more drivers register for a race session than the track and/or series allows, the race will be split into fields of as close to equal number of cars as possible.

5.1.2.3. Drivers are placed in a race based primarily on their iRatings at the time of the race start.

5.1.2.4. Other factors can be and are taken into account for splitting races, as FIRST and iRacing see fit in order to improve the online competition environment.

5.1.3. Field Sizes and Race Lengths

5.1.3.1. Races will have a limited number of drivers as determined by the FIRST Competition Board in order to ensure safe and competitive racing within each License Class. The following table provides guidelines for STANDARD series field sizes and race lengths by license class. FIRST reserves the right, however, to adjust field sizes and race lengths as it deems necessary to optimize competition. (See Table 5.1)

Table 5.1

License Class	Minimum Drivers	Maximum Drivers	Minimum Race Length
Rookie	6	12	20 Minutes
Class "D"	8	16	30 Minutes
Class "C"	8	20	45 Minutes
Class "B"	8	30	60 Minutes
Class "A"	8	30	60 Minutes
Pro-Series	12	32	60 Minutes

5.1.4. Warm-up

5.1.4.1. Once race groups are parsed and the session has begun, each race will have a warm-up period of approximately 5 minutes.

5.1.4.2. Once warm-up is complete, the checkered flag will be displayed. After 10 seconds, the pre-gridding process will commence.

5.1.5. Gridding

5.1.5.1. Each driver will have 60 seconds to place his car on the starting grid.

5.1.5.2. Any driver not gridding his car within the 60 second time limit must start the race from his/her pit box, with a possible hold from Race Control to ensure safe entry onto the track.

5.1.5.3. The 60-second period for gridding time may be cut short if all drivers have entered their cars. When this occurs, Race Control will proceed directly to starting.

5.1.6. Starting

5.1.6.1. Standard road race starts will be from a standing start.

5.1.6.2. The countdown to the start of the race will be signified by the illumination of four (4) red lights. After a short delay, the 4 lights will turn green simultaneously, signifying the start of the race.

5.1.6.3. Any motion by a car prior to the display of the green flag/lights may be viewed by Race Control as a jumped start and result in a black flag Stop-and-Go penalty.

5.1.7. Flag Signals

5.1.7.1. Green Flag – Indicates the start of a race, clear track condition, and/or the cancellation of a previous flag condition.

5.1.7.2. White Flag – When displayed at start/finish line, indicates the start of the last lap and will be displayed to the leader first and then to the remainder of the Competitors.

5.1.7.3. Checkered Flag – Indicates the end of a session, warm-up period, or end of the race.

5.1.7.4. Yellow Flag – When displayed motionlessly (Standing Yellow), indicates danger, no passing, be prepared to slow down. When displayed with motion (Waving Yellow), indicates extreme danger, no passing, be prepared to slow down, track may be partially or completely blocked. In either case, Competitors may not pass until the Yellow flag is removed, as indicated by the absence of the Yellow flag and/or presence of the Green flag at the next corner station.

5.1.7.5. Blue Flag (blue with diagonal yellow stripe) – Indicates faster cars are approaching. This flag is informational only. In all cases, it is the responsibility of the faster car to safely overtake the slower car. It is the responsibility of the slower car to maintain a consistent line. It is strongly recommended that a slower car being lapped makes every reasonable effort to facilitate a safe pass.

5.1.7.6. Black Flag (furled) – When displayed furled, indicates a warning from Race Control and may require action, such as slowing on course, to avoid an in-session penalty.

5.1.7.7. Black Flag – When displayed unfurled, indicates an in-session penalty from Race Control, return to your pit box to serve your penalty. When displayed with a white "X," indicates disqualification from the session.

5.1.7.8. Failure to comply with any Flag Signal may result in a Black Flag Penalty being assessed by Race Control.

5.1.8. Black Flag Rules

5.1.8.1. Race Control may assess three types of Black Flag Penalties:

5.1.8.1.1. Stop-and-Go – requires the penalized driver to return to his/her pit box and come to a complete stop inside the box before rejoining the race.

5.1.8.1.2. Stop-and-Hold – requires the penalized driver to return to his/her pit box and come to a complete stop inside the box. Race Control will then hold the driver for a specific duration of time before releasing him/her to rejoin the race.

5.1.8.1.3. Disqualification -- Upon disqualification, a driver will have 30 seconds to pull off of the racing line and exit the session, after which Race Control will automatically remove the disqualified driver. Race Control will immediately remove from the session any driver disqualified for reckless driving.

5.1.8.2. If a driver is assessed a black flag penalty by Race Control in any session, he/she must return to pits to serve the penalty. Although the driver's lap count will continue uninterrupted, official lap times will not be recorded until the driver has served his/her penalty.

5.1.8.3. The driver may not use the Enter/Exit/Tow Car control (also known as "Reset") to return to the pits to serve a Black Flag penalty during a Race session. (Using Enter/Exit/Tow Car to clear Black Flags is allowed as a convenience only in Testing, Practice, Qualifying and Time Trials).

5.1.8.4. Failure to return to the pits and serve a black flag penalty within 4 laps of notification from Race Control will result in disqualification.

5.1.9. Yellow Flag Procedures

5.1.9.1. On road courses, if a local yellow flag is displayed, passing is prohibited until the flag is no longer displayed or is replaced by a green flag.

5.1.9.2. Drivers found to have passed under a local yellow may be assessed a black flag Stop-and-Go penalty by Race Control.

5.1.9.3. In the event of a full-course caution, a yellow flag will be displayed at start/finish and all corner stations. Race Control will freeze the running order and send the pace car out to pick up the race leader. Drivers must comply with instructions from Race Control regarding where to line up behind the pace car. Failure to do so will result in the driver being sent to the end of the longest pace line for the restart.

5.1.10. Pitting Procedures

5.1.10.1. For Race Control purposes, pit lane shall be defined by a pair of yellow cones, one on each side of the lane, indicating the start of pit lane and a pair of green cones, one on each side of the lane, indicating the end of pit lane.

5.1.10.2. Where possible, every pit area will include three individual lanes. In order from the inside pit wall, they are – the pit box or pit stall lane (where a driver's crew stands), the acceleration/deceleration lane and a fast lane.

5.1.10.3. When leaving his/her pit stall, a driver shall as quickly as is practicable enter the acceleration/deceleration lane in order to avoid incidental contact with cars being automatically placed into nearby pit stalls. Similarly, a driver shall remain in the acceleration/deceleration lane until just prior to entering his/her pit stall in order to avoid incidental contact with cars being automatically placed into nearby pit stalls.

5.1.10.4. Pit lane speed limits are in place for all series and all official sessions. Drivers must slow to the posted pit lane speed limit prior to passing through the two yellow cones that mark the entrance to pit lane, and drivers may not accelerate above the pit lane speed limit until after passing through the two green cones that mark the exit of pit lane. Failure to obey the posted pit lane speed limit will result in a 15-second black flag Stop-and-Hold penalty.

5.1.10.5. At tracks with defined pit lane entry and exit, as indicated by existing painted lines, barriers and/or cones, drivers must observe and obey such demarcations. Failure to do so on entry may result in a 15-second black flag Stop-and-Hold penalty. Failure to do so on exit may result in a black flag Stop-and-Go penalty.

5.1.10.6. A driver's car must be inside his/her assigned pit box to serve a penalty or receive pit service. All penalties are served after pit service has been completed.

5.1.10.7. The exit of pit lane may be closed, as indicated by Race Control. This closure may occur at the beginning of a race and continue until after the race has started. Leaving a closed pit lane under green flag conditions will result in a Stop-and-Go penalty.

5.1.10.8. A driver may call for a tow to the pits at any point during a race by pressing the "Enter/Exit/Tow Car" control, which will move the driver forward around the track to his/her pit, where they will be held for some amount of time that represents a tow vehicle returning the driver's car to the pits. The time the tow takes is based on how far forward around the track the driver's car is being towed, so that the driver is neither gaining nor losing track position to the other competitors, plus a base penalty time for calling for a tow. If the tow takes a driver across the start/finish line to his/her pit stall, the driver will be scored for that lap after the tow completes. Once the tow is complete, the driver's pit crew may complete any requested pit work and attempt to repair the car, and any pending penalties will be served.

5.1.10.9. The duration of a tow is based on minimizing advantage gained or lost relative to other competitors on track regardless of where on the track a tow is called for. To this end, the duration of the tow is longer while a full course caution is in effect and competitors on track are travelling at pacing speeds than during green flag racing when competitors are at full racing speed. Any tow in progress will lengthen or shorten the remaining time appropriately if a full course caution begins or ends while still towing.

5.1.10.10. Exiting a car or disconnecting from the server while driving is equivalent to requesting a tow. The tow continues while the driver is out of his/her car or disconnected and trying to rejoin. The driver may re-enter his/her car at any time during or after the tow, but will still have to wait for the tow to complete before performing pit crew actions or continuing the race.

5.1.10.11. In Rookie and Class D series, the first request for a tow during the race will be of a slightly shorter duration than a regular tow, and the driver's car will be fully repaired and restored by the tow. Any subsequent requests for a tow will be regular tows with a normal tow duration and no repairing or restoration of the car will occur, leaving any repairs to the pit crew to attempt. In Class C, B, A, and Pro there are no faster tows, only regular tows.

5.1.10.12. A driver may pit under power, without pressing "Enter/Exit/Tow Car," as often as he/she chooses, for the purposes of changing tires, refueling, repairing, and/or serving penalties.

5.1.11. Reckless Driving

5.1.11.1. Driving in the opposite direction of race traffic during any official session will be viewed by Race Control as deliberate reckless driving. A furled black flag warning will be displayed immediately. Failure to comply promptly will result in disqualification.

5.1.11.2. Driving in the opposite direction of race traffic during a post-race cool-down period will result in a one-lap penalty, assessed in the final scoring. At the conclusion of any multi-car session, drivers must either return safely to pit lane or bring their car to a safe stop off the racing surface so as not to create an incident hazard for other competitors still at speed.

5.1.11.3. Other deliberate reckless driving, including avoidable contact and intentional wrecking, is prohibited. Competitors who believe that they have been victims of such action – and those competitors who believe that they have witnessed such action – are strongly encouraged to file Protests in accordance with Section 8 of the FIRST Sporting Code.

5.1.12. Other Penalties

5.1.12.1. Cutting the Course – Drivers gaining an advantage by following a course configuration other than the one specified for the event will be assessed a black flag Stop-and-Hold penalty by Race Control, with the duration of the hold being equal to the illegally gained time advantage plus 15 seconds. Any other cutting the course infractions will result in a furled black flag warning and the driver will have 15 seconds to slow down and comply before being assessed a black flag Stop-and-Hold penalty by Race Control, with the duration of the hold being equal to the illegally gained time advantage plus 15 seconds.

5.1.12.2. Blocking – Any deviation by a driver from his or her racing line, which impedes the forward progress of a following car, will be considered blocking and may be grounds for Protest in accordance with Section 8 of the FIRST Sporting Code.

5.1.12.3. Intentional actions to cause a caution period – drivers intentionally stopping on or off the racing surface to intentionally bring out a caution period for their benefit or the benefit of another driver – are forbidden and subject to adverse administrative and /or punitive actions.

5.1.12.4. Drivers may not use the enter/exit/tow car to gain positions during a race. This includes driving your damaged vehicle to your pit box then exiting the pit box and subsequently using the enter/exit/tow car function to move forward around the track to complete laps and pass competitors who've since retired or disconnected from the race session. Affected drivers may submit a protest in accordance with Section 8.

5.1.12.5. Drivers may not drive damaged vehicles on the apron at reduced speeds with the intent of gaining positions from drivers that have retired or disconnected due to damaged race cars. The intent of this action is contradictory to the spirit of competition and creates an unsafe environment for the remaining drivers not damaged and still racing. This may be protested in accordance with Section 8.

5.1.13. Official Completion

5.1.13.1. Unless otherwise stated in the Supplementary Regulations, all races will be run until the leader has completed the advertised distance. If unforeseen circumstances prevent the completion of the advertised distance and/or it is impractical to continue the race within a reasonable time after it has been stopped, the race will be considered officially complete if the halfway mark has been reached by the leader.

5.1.13.2. In the event that a competitor disconnects from the service for any reason (e.g., interruption of Internet service or PC failure), the competitor may rejoin the race from his/her pit stall if he/she has not already been towed to the pits (by pressing "Enter/Exit/Tow Car") during the race. Rejoining the race after disconnection will be considered by Race Control as a tow to the pits (see Pitting Procedures, section 5.1.10.7). The competitor will rejoin with a lap count equal to that scored at the time of disconnection. If the competitor fails to rejoin prior to the end of the race, he/she will be scored as a DNF with a lap total equal to the number of laps completed at the time of disconnection.

5.1.13.3. In the event of race server failure or an interruption to the entire iRacing.com service, whether through loss of power, equipment failure, natural disaster or any other cause, official race results, including overall session and driver-specific performance data (including but not limited to points, iRating changes, incidents and lap times), will stand, unless FIRST publishes an official notification to the contrary to http://members.iracing.com.

5.2. Ovals

5.2.1. Registration

5.2.1.1. All FIRST-sanctioned races are available for registration 30 Minutes prior to the start of the event.

5.2.1.2. A timer will be visible in the Member Website Race Panel counting down to the start of the Race Session.

5.2.1.3. Anytime between the opening of registration and 2 minutes prior to the session start time, drivers may withdraw from the Race Session without a point or iRating penalty.

5.2.1.4. Withdrawing from a Race Session with 2 minutes or fewer left on the countdown timer may result in a forfeit.

5.2.1.5. Any driver forfeiting a race will be credited with a last-place finish and earn 0 points for that race. The race will be counted in the driver's Race Week Average (see RACE WEEK POINTS, section 4.1.6.4 above)

5.2.1.6. Any Driver forfeiting a race will be credited with a last-place finish and his/her iRating will reflect a negative change equal to a last place finish.

5.2.2. Field Sizes and Race Lengths

5.2.2.1. Races will have a limited number of drivers as determined by the FIRST Competition Board in order to ensure safe and competitive racing within each License Class. The following table provides guidelines for STANDARD series field sizes and race lengths by license class. FIRST reserves the right, however, to adjust field sizes and race lengths as it deems necessary to optimize competition. (See Table 5.2)

Table 5.2

License Class	Minimum Drivers	Maximum Drivers	Minimum Race Length
Rookie	6	12	40 Laps
Class "D"	8	16	50 Laps
Class "C"	8	20	60 Laps
Class "B"	8	30	60 Minutes
Class "A"	8	30	60 Minutes
Pro-Series	12	32	60 Minutes

5.2.3. Race Splits

5.2.3.1. FIRST and iRacing.com seek to have similarly skilled drivers racing together in each event.

5.2.3.2. Should more drivers register for a race session than the track and/or series allows, the race will be split into fields of as close to equal number of cars as possible.

5.2.3.3. Drivers are placed in a race based primarily on their iRatings at the time of the race start.

5.2.3.4. Other factors can be and are taken into account for splitting races, as FIRST and iRacing see fit in order to improve the online competition environment.

5.2.4. Warm-up

5.2.4.1. Once race groups are parsed and the session has begun, each race will have a warm-up period of approximately 5 minutes.

5.2.4.2. Once warm-up is complete, the checkered flag will be displayed. After 10 seconds, the pre-gridding process will commence.

5.2.5. Gridding

5.2.5.1. Each driver will have 60 seconds to place his car on the starting grid.

5.2.5.2. Any driver not gridding his car within the 60 second time limit must start the race from his/her pit box, with a possible hold from Race Control to ensure safe entry onto the track.

5.2.6. Starting

5.2.6.1. Standard oval race starts will be in the form of a rolling start.

5.2.6.2. Once all drivers are on the grid, the pace car will lead the field around the track and exit the course as late as possible to enter pit lane.

5.2.6.3. As the front row of cars approach the start/finish line, the green flag will be shown, signifying the start of the race.

5.2.6.4. Drivers shall not pass cars in their own pacing line on the left hand side before the start/finish line. Drivers attempting to improve their position by passing on the left-hand side before the start/finish line will be assessed a black flag Stop-and-Go penalty by Race Control.

5.2.6.5. The leader of the second pace line may not pass the leader of the first pace line (pole position) before the start/finish line. Doing so will result in a black flag Stop-and-Go penalty.

5.2.7. Flag Signals

5.2.7.1. Green Flag – Indicates the start of a race, clear track condition, and/or the cancellation of a previous flag condition.

5.2.7.2. White Flag – When displayed at start/finish line, indicates the start of the last lap and will be displayed to the leader first and then to the remainder of the Competitors.

5.2.7.3. Checkered Flag – Indicates the end of a session warm-up period, or end of the race

5.2.7.4. Yellow Flag – When displayed, indicates caution, danger, no passing, be prepared to slow down. Line up behind the pace car as instructed by Race Control. Competitors may not pass until the Yellow flag is removed and the green flag is displayed, signifying a restart.

5.2.7.5. Blue Flag (blue with diagonal yellow stripe) – Indicates lead-lap cars are approaching, give way. This flag is informational only. In all cases, it is the responsibility of the faster car to safely overtake the slower car. It is the responsibility of the slower car to maintain a consistent line. It is strongly recommended that a slower car being lapped makes every reasonable effort to facilitate a safe pass.

5.2.7.6. Black Flag (furled) – When displayed furled, indicates a warning from Race Control and may require action, such as slowing on course, to avoid an in-session penalty.

5.2.7.7. Black Flag – When displayed unfurled, indicates an in-session penalty from Race Control, return to your pit box to serve your penalty. When displayed with a white "X," indicates disqualification from the session.

5.2.8. Black Flag Rules

5.2.8.1. Race Control may assess three types of Black Flag Penalties:

5.2.8.1.1. Stop-and-Go – requires the penalized driver to return to his/her pit box and come to a complete stop inside the box before rejoining the race.

5.2.8.1.2. Stop-and-Hold – requires the penalized driver to return to his/her pit box and come to a complete stop inside the box. Race Control will then hold the driver for a specific duration of time before releasing him/her to rejoin the race.

5.2.8.1.3. Disqualification -- Upon disqualification, a driver will have 30 seconds to pull off of the racing line and exit the session, after which Race Control will automatically remove the disqualified driver. Race Control will immediately remove from the session any driver disqualified for reckless driving.

5.2.8.2. If a driver is assessed a black flag penalty by Race Control in any session, he/she must return to pit lane to serve the penalty. Although the driver's lap count will continue uninterrupted, official lap times will not be recorded until the driver has served his/her penalty.

5.2.8.3. The driver may not use the Enter/Exit/Tow Car control (also known as "Reset") to return to the pits to serve a Black Flag penalty during a Race session. (Using Enter/Exit/Tow Car to clear Black Flags is allowed as a convenience only in Testing, Practice, Qualifying and Time Trials).

5.2.8.4. Failure to return to the pits and serve a black flag penalty within 4 laps of notification from Race Control will result in disqualification.

5.2.9. Yellow Flag Procedures

5.2.9.1. On ovals, a yellow flag will signal a full-course caution. The pacing order will be frozen at the moment the full-course caution begins. Cars involved in causing the caution or otherwise seen as out of control may, however, not be awarded a place in the pacing order until they are detected to be on course and under control. Race Control will instruct the leader to follow the pace car. All other drivers must line up in single file in accordance with instructions from Race Control. Up/down arrows will be shown to assist drivers in preparation for a restart. Failure to line up correctly by the time a driver attempts a pit entry or the race restarts will result in the driver receiving a black flag penalty.

5.2.9.2. While pacing during a full-course caution, Race Control will signify two laps to go, then one lap to go until the green flag restart.

5.2.9.3. When there is one lap of pacing to go until the green flag restart, Race Control may restructure the pace lines in preparation for the restart. If there will be 10 or fewer laps remaining in the race from the restart, the restart will be single file; cars that are not on the lead lap will be shuffled down the pacing order, behind cars that are on the lead lap. If there are more than 10 laps remaining, the restart will be double file if there are any cars not on the lead lap. Lapped cars will line up on the inside pace line, and lead-lap cars will line up on the outside pace line.

5.2.10. Pit Stop Procedures

5.2.10.1. For Race Control purposes, pit lane shall be defined by a pair of yellow cones, one on each side of the lane, indicating the start of pit lane and a pair of green cones, one on each side of the lane, indicating the end of pit lane.

5.2.10.2. Where possible, every pit area will include three individual lanes. In order from the inside pit wall, they are – the pit box or pit stall lane (where a driver's crew stands), the acceleration/deceleration lane and a fast lane.

5.2.10.3. When leaving his/her pit stall, a driver shall as quickly as is practicable enter the acceleration/deceleration lane in order to avoid incidental contact with cars being automatically placed into nearby pit stalls. Similarly, a driver shall remain in the acceleration/deceleration lane until just prior to entering his/her pit stall in order to avoid incidental contact with cars being automatically placed into nearby pit stalls.

5.2.10.4. Pit lane speed limits are in place for all series and all official sessions. Drivers must slow to the posted pit lane speed limit prior to passing through the two yellow cones that mark the entrance to pit lane, and drivers may not accelerate above the pit lane speed limit until after passing through the two green cones that mark the exit of pit lane. Failure to obey the posted pit lane speed limit will result in a 15-second black flag Stop-and-Hold penalty when the violation happens under green flag conditions. Failure to obey the posted pit lane speed limit under full-course caution conditions will result in the driver being sent to the end of the longest line for the restart.

5.2.10.5. At tracks with defined pit lane entry and exit, as indicated by existing painted lines, barriers and/or cones, drivers must observe and obey such demarcations. Failure to do so on entry may result in a 15-second black flag Stop-and-Hold penalty. Failure to do so on exit may result in a black flag Stop-and-Go penalty. Failure to follow the pit-entry and pit-exit procedures during a full-course caution will result in the driver being sent to the end of the longest line for the restart.

5.2.10.6. A driver's car must be inside his/her assigned pit box to serve a penalty or receive pit service. All penalties are served after pit service has been completed.

5.2.10.7. When a full-course caution begins, Race Control will indicate the closure of all pit lane entrances. Pit lane will open for cars on the lead lap on their first lap after crossing the start/finish line under full-course caution. Pit lane will open for lapped cars on their second lap after crossing the start/finish line under full-course caution. Entering a closed pit lane will result in the driver being sent to the end of the longest pacing line for the restart.

5.2.10.8. The exit of pit lane may be closed, as indicated by Race Control. This closure can occur at the beginning of a race and continue until after the race has started, or it can occur when a full-course caution is in progress and the pacing field is passing the pit exit. Leaving pit lane while the exit is closed under green-flag conditions will result in a Stop-and-Go penalty. Leaving pit lane while the exit is closed during a full-course caution will result in the driver being sent to the end of the longest pacing line for the restart.

5.2.10.9. A driver may call for a tow to the pits at any point during a race by pressing the "Enter/Exit/Tow Car" control, which will move the driver forward around the track to his/her pit, where they will be held for some amount of time that represents a tow vehicle returning the driver's car to the pits. The time the tow takes is based on how far forward around the track the driver's car is being towed, so that the driver is neither gaining nor losing track position to the other competitors, plus a base penalty time for calling for a tow. If the tow takes a driver across the start/finish line to his/her pit stall, the driver will be scored for that lap after the tow completes. Once the tow is complete, the driver's pit crew may complete any requested pit work and attempt to repair the car, and any pending penalties will be served.

5.2.10.10. The duration of a tow is based on minimizing advantage gained or lost relative to other competitors on track regardless of where on the track a tow is called for. To this end, the duration of the tow is longer while a full course caution is in effect and competitors on track are travelling at pacing speeds than during green flag racing when competitors are at full racing speed. Any tow in progress will lengthen or shorten the remaining time appropriately if a full course caution begins or ends while still towing.

5.2.10.11. Exiting a car or disconnecting from the server while driving is equivalent to requesting a tow. The tow continues while the driver is out of his/her car or disconnected and trying to rejoin. The driver may re-enter his/her car at any time during or after the tow, but will still have to wait for the tow to complete before performing pit crew actions or continuing the race.

5.2.10.12. In Rookie and Class D series, the first request for a tow during the race will be of a slightly shorter duration than a regular tow, and the driver's car will be fully repaired and restored by the tow. Any subsequent requests for a tow will be regular tows with a normal tow duration and no repairing or restoration of the car will occur, leaving any repairs to the pit crew to attempt. In Class C, B, A, and Pro there are no faster tows, only regular tows.

5.2.10.13. A driver may pit under power, without pressing "Enter/Exit/Tow Car," as often as he/she chooses, for the purposes of changing tires, refueling, repairing, and/or serving penalties.

5.2.11. Reckless Driving

5.2.11.1. Driving in the opposite direction of race traffic during any official session will be viewed by Race Control as deliberate reckless driving. A furled black flag warning will be displayed immediately. Failure to comply promptly will result in disqualification.

5.2.11.2. Driving in the opposite direction of race traffic during a post-race cool-down period will result in a one-lap penalty. At the conclusion of any multi-car session, drivers must either return safely to pit lane or bring their car to a safe stop off the racing surface so as not to create an incident hazard for other competitors still at speed.

5.2.11.3. Other deliberate reckless driving, including avoidable contact and intentional wrecking, is prohibited. Competitors who believe that they have been victims of such action – and those competitors who believe that they have witnessed such action – are strongly encouraged to file Protests in accordance with Section 8 of the FIRST Sporting Code.

5.2.12. Other Penalties

5.2.12.1. Cutting the Course – Drivers gaining an advantage by following a course configuration other than the one specified for the event will be assessed a black flag Stop-and-Hold penalty by Race Control, with the duration of the hold being equal to the illegally gained time advantage plus 15 seconds. Any other cutting the course infractions will result in a furled black flag warning, and the driver will have 15 seconds to slow down and comply before being assessed a black flag Stop-and-Hold penalty by Race Control, with the duration of the hold being equal to the illegally gained time advantage plus 15 seconds.

5.2.12.2. Blocking – Any deviation by a driver from his or her racing line, which impedes the forward progress of a following car, will be considered blocking and may be grounds for Protest in accordance with Section 8 of the FIRST Sporting Code.

5.2.12.3. Intentional actions to cause a caution period – drivers intentionally stopping on or off the racing surface to intentionally bring out a caution period for their benefit or the benefit of another driver – are forbidden and subject to adverse administrative and /or punitive actions.

5.2.12.4. Drivers may not use the enter/exit/tow car to gain positions during a race. This includes driving your damaged vehicle to your pit box then exiting the pit box and subsequently using the enter/exit/tow car function to move forward around the track to complete laps and pass competitors who've since retired or disconnected from the race session. Affected drivers may submit a protest in accordance with Section 8.

5.2.12.5. Drivers may not drive damaged vehicles on the apron at reduced speeds with the intent of gaining positions from drivers that have retired or disconnected due to damaged race cars. The intent of this action is contradictory to the spirit of competition and creates an unsafe environment for the remaining drivers not damaged and still racing. This may be protested in accordance with Section 8.

5.2.13. Official Completion

5.2.13.1. Unless otherwise stated in the Supplementary Regulations, all races will be run until the leader has completed the advertised distance. If unforeseen circumstances prevent the completion of the advertised distance and/or it is impractical to continue the race within a reasonable time after it has been stopped, the race will be considered officially complete if the halfway mark has been reached by the leader.

5.2.13.2. In the event that a competitor disconnects from the service for any reason (e.g., interruption of Internet service or PC failure), the competitor may rejoin the race from his/her pit stall if he/she has not already been towed to the pits (by pressing "Enter/Exit/Tow Car") during the race. Rejoining the race after disconnection will be considered by Race Control as a tow to the pits (see Pitting Procedures, section 5.2.10.7). The competitor will rejoin with a lap count equal to that scored at the time of disconnection. If the competitor fails to rejoin prior to the end of the race, he/she will be scored as a DNF with a lap total equal to the number of laps completed at the time of disconnection.

5.2.13.3. In the event of race server failure or an interruption to the entire iRacing.com service, whether through loss of power, equipment failure, natural disaster or any other cause, official race results, including overall session and driver-specific performance data (including but not limited to points, iRating changes, incidents and lap times), will stand, unless FIRST publishes an official notification to the contrary to http://members.iracing.com.

6. iRacing.com Clubs

6.1. Principle

6.1.1. Clubs are a focal point of iRacing.com's global service. Club championships are structured in a way that necessitates working together in order to successfully compete for the World Cup of iRacing.

6.2. Club Assignments

6.2.1. Members residing in the Continental United States of America will be assigned to clubs on a geographical basis by state.

6.2.2. Members residing outside of the Continental United States will be assigned to clubs on a geographical basis by Country.

6.3. Club Names

6.3.1. The following are the initial clubs within FIRST.

Table 6.3

Northeastern Region	Mid-Atlantic Region	Southeastern Region	Central Region
Massachusetts	Pennsylvania	Georgia	Illinois
New England	Virginias	Florida	Indiana
Connecticut	Atlantic	Mid-South	Michigan
New York	New Jersey	Carolina	Midwest
Eastern Canada	Ohio	South America	Texas
			Plains

Pacific Region	Western European Region	Central European Region
West	England	Italy
Northwest	Celtic	International
California	Iberia	DE-AT-CH
Australia	France	Scandinavia
Western Canada	Benelux	

6.4. Club Geography

6.4.1. Clubs will be assigned to seven Regions. (See Table 6.3)

6.4.2. See Annex A for breakdown of clubs.

6.5. Club Structure

6.5.1. Each Region may have a Liaison to represent his/her region in interactions with the FIRST Competition Board.

6.5.2. The FIRST Competition Board shall appoint a Regional Liaison for each new club. Provided the appointee accepts this volunteer position, he/she shall oversee all region business, including the administration of fair and open elections for any additional official regional positions.

6.5.3. FIRST shall annually publish to http://members.iracing.com the iRacing.com Club Guide, which will include recommended club roles, election processes and miscellaneous other policies.

6.5.4. If a Regional Liaison chooses to step down, he/she is responsible to alert the FIRST Competition Board immediately, and the Board will appoint a new Regional Liaison at its earliest convenience.

6.5.5. FIRST reserves the right to replace any Regional Liaison at any time if it believes such action is in the best interest of the membership and/or internet racing.

7. Penalties

7.1. Penalties

7.1.1. Any breach of this Official Sporting Code, or the Appendices thereto, or any Supplementary Regulations by any member of iRacing may result in a penalty for said member. Penalties may be determined by the FIRST Chief Steward, which will always be an iRacing official and will be appointed by FIRST. The decisions of the FIRST Chief Steward become immediately binding regardless of pending appeals. The penalty will remain in effect until the appeal process has concluded. All appeals are to be made according to the procedure, and will be subject to the limitations, set forth in Section 9 of this document (Appeals).

7.2. Breach of Rules

7.2.1. Any of the following offenses in addition to any offenses referred to previously, shall be deemed to be a breach of rules:

7.2.1.1. Any attempt, direct or indirect, to bribe any person having official duties in relation to a competition or being employed in any manner in connection with iRacing or FIRST in connection with a competition and the acceptance of, or offer to accept, any bribe by such employee or official.

7.2.1.2. Any action having as its object to illegally alter the simulation, content, cars, tracks or any aspects of the software to gain unfair competitive advantage.

7.2.1.3. Any fraudulent conduct or any act prejudicial to the interests of any competition or to the interests of internet racing in general.

7.3. Application of Penalties

7.3.1. Penalties may be applied as follows:

7.3.1.1. Warning. (May not be appealed)

7.3.1.2. Racing time penalty, including in-session penalties (e.g., stop-and-go), as well as post-event timing and scoring adjustments. (May not be appealed)

7.3.1.3. Race Disqualification: (May not be appealed)

7.3.1.4. Suspension from competition and/or communications with other members within the service for a specific period of time; includes racing, open practice, qualifying sessions, open chat and forums. (May be appealed in accordance with Section 9)

7.3.1.5. Suspension of membership for a specific period of time. May be appealed in accordance with Section 9)

7.3.1.6. Permanent revocation of membership. (May be appealed in accordance with Section 9)

7.3.1.7. Any other penalty deemed appropriate by the FIRST Competition Board. (May be appealed in accordance with Section 9)

7.3.2. If a member is assessed a probation or suspension, he or she must serve the full term of the penalty while his or her iRacing membership is active.

7.3.3. Regardless of any Protests, Appeals or Penalties assessed, iRatings, ttRatings and Safety Ratings will not be adjusted.

7.4. Loss of Awards

7.4.1. Any competitor or member penalized in any way may lose the right to receive awards granted for a racing or driving competition, series competition or club competition at the sole discretion of iRacing and/or FIRST.

7.4.2. iRacing and/or FIRST retains the right to withhold monetary awards from competitors if found that he/she has violated the Terms of Service, The end User License Agreement, Code of Conduct, and/or This Official FIRST Sporting Code.

7.5. Publication of Penalties

7.5.1. iRacing and/or FIRST shall have the right to publish the name of any member assessed a penalty, as well as the nature of the infraction or violation and any associated penalties, on its member website or any other affiliated public forum.

7.6. Remission of Penalties

7.6.1. iRacing or FIRST shall have the right to remit the unexpired period of disqualification, suspension or revocation.

8. Protests

8.1. Who may Protest

8.1.1. The right to protest shall rest with any iRacing member who officially takes part in the competition in question or feels any part of the Sporting Code or official rules of iRacing or FIRST have been violated. Each, alone, may protest any decision, act, or omission of iRacing, FIRST, an official, driver, or other person connected to the competition which the protestor believes is unfair or in violation of the Sporting Code or other official regulations or rules of iRacing or FIRST.

8.2. Lodging a Protest

8.2.1. A Protest must be made in writing, specifying which sections of Sporting Code, racing rules, club rules, series rules or any official iRacing or FIRST rules have been violated. Protests should include the exact infraction and why it is believed a violation has occurred. The event needs to be clearly identified including time and date it occurred. Written protests must be addressed to "FIRST Chief Steward" and submitted to Protest@iRacing.com. This is the only place to formally lodge a protest. Protests need to be made within 7 days of the decision, infraction or violation that is being protested. Any evidence, data, recordings or third party accounts are welcome and encouraged to be submitted with protests.

8.2.2. Protest submitted regarding on track incidents should be accompanied by a replay of the on track incident in question.

8.2.3. Below is an example of a properly formatted Protest:

> Session ID: 1247836/54220
> Date: 2008-05-08 11:00 pm Sporting Code Section: 5.5.11 Driver: Joe Smith Description/Explanation of Protest: On lap 9 of the race, Joe Smith typed in text chat ....
> Accompanying Attachments: chat_text.jpg, Incident.rpy

8.3. Review of Protest

8.3.1. iRacing shall review the protest as soon as practical after the protest is lodged. Affected parties may be notified about the protest and judgment of the protest. iRacing shall review all evidence and be entitled to discuss the incident with other witnesses or parties involved or to gather additional evidence.

8.4. Judgment

8.4.1. All parties concerned shall be bound by the decision given, subject only to appeal as provided in section 9.

8.5. Reasonableness

8.5.1. It is expected that protests shall be reasonable, logical, and based on sound evidence, thus well-founded. Nevertheless, a well founded protest may still be defined as one upon which reasonable people may differ.

8.5.2. Regardless of the outcome of any adjudication, FIRST may deem a protest to be frivolous if it is found by the FIRST Competition Board not to be reasonable, logical and based on sound evidence. FIRST reserves the right to assess a penalty to any member filing a frivolous protest.

8.6. Steward's Review

8.6.1. The FIRST Chief Steward may investigate any competitor against whom one or more protests have been filed, regardless of the outcome of any protests against or appeals by that competitor.

8.6.2. Investigations that are inconclusive will be logged as "Noted Incidents" in the driver's official record. Noted Incidents are administrative records, not infractions or penalties, and may not be appealed.

8.6.3. Accumulation by a competitor of multiple "Noted Incidents" will result in a Steward's Review of that competitor's driving record.

9. Appeals

9.1. Right to Appeal

9.1.1. Any member assessed a penalty or named as a party to a protest, shall have the right to appeal any decision or penalty imposed by the FIRST Chief Steward, the FIRST Competition Board, iRacing.com or FIRST.

9.1.2. All iRacing.com members are afforded one free appeal for each 12-week racing season. FIRST reserves the right to charge members an administration fee for additional appeals.

9.2. Jurisdiction

9.2.1. The Chairman of FIRST will appoint a three-member Appeals Committee (and one alternate to serve in the event that one of the primary members is unavailable) each year to review and render a final decision on any appeals filed.

9.3. Well-Founded Appeals

9.3.1. To be considered by the Appeals Committee, an appeal must be well-founded. An appeal shall be reasonable, logical and based on sound evidence, though reasonable people may differ on the interpretation of the evidence.

9.3.2. Regardless of the outcome of any adjudication, the Appeals Committee may deem an appeal to be frivolous if it is found by the Appeals Committee not to be reasonable, logical and based on sound evidence. FIRST reserves the right to assess a penalty to any member filing a frivolous appeal.

9.4. Hearing Appeals

9.4.1. All properly filed appeals shall be reviewed by the Appeals Committee. It may at its discretion, require the appellant to submit any additional evidence it deems necessary for an equitable decision; hear direct evidence from a person deemed to have pertinent information or data; or seek information from any source it desires. The Appeals Committee shall make every effort to render its final decision within 30 days of its receipt of the Notice of Appeal.

9.5. Initiating an Appeal

9.5.1. Appeals must be made in writing, specifically asking for an appeal, specifying the exact nature of the appeal and why it is believed an appeal is warranted, along with all evidence to support the appeal. Written appeals must be addressed to "Appeals Committee-iRacing" and submitted to Appeal@iRacing.com. This is the only place to formally make an appeal. Appeals must be submitted within seven days of the penalty or decision being appealed. Any evidence, data, recordings or third party accounts are welcome and encouraged to be submitted with appeal. "Intent to Appeal" or other informal appeals of any kind will not be accepted.

9.5.2. Below is an example of a properly formatted Appeal:
Case #: CAS-2816-XSWYLN
Sporting Code Section: 4.1.3.1 Driver: Joe Smith Grounds for and Description of Appeal: I feel the wrong decision was made in this case because ...
Accompanying Attachments:
chat_text.jpg

9.6. Bad Faith Appeal

9.6.1. If the Appeals Committee determines that the appellant has acted in bad faith or in an harassing manner, it may deem such conduct a breach of the Sporting Code and impose a penalty as listed above.

9.7. Notification and Final Appeal Decision

9.7.1. The Appeals Committee will notify the appellant of its final decision as soon as possible after the decision is rendered. iRacing.com and FIRST shall also have the right to publish the appeal to other or all iRacing.com members. Members or any persons shall have no right of action against the Appeals Committee, iRacing.com or FIRST. The final appeal decision shall be final and binding with no other right to appeal.

9.7.2. All iRacing.com members expressly agree not to initiate or maintain claims, suits or actions of any kind, including without limitation arbitration proceedings, against iRacing.com, FIRST or anyone acting on behalf of these organizations, with respect to any final appeal decision.

9.7.3. All iRacing.com members expressly agree that if any member initiates or maintains any claim, suit or action in violation of the above provision, that member will reimburse iRacing.com for all costs and expenses relating to the claim, suit or action, including attorneys' fees, and that such amount represents damages and not a penalty against the member.

10. Records

10.1. All competition records, data and statistics are to be considered unofficial until verified in writing by an authorized official of FIRST or iRacing.com.

11. Hosted Sessions

11.1. Hosted Races

11.1.1. All member hosted sessions are unofficial. Safety Rating and iRating will not be gained or lost during any member hosted session.

11.1.2. Points will be awarded in hosted races and will be displayed in the results of these sessions, however, iRacing will not track championship points.

11.1.3. Club points shown in results are not factored into the World Cup of iRacing standings.

11.1.4. Hosted races may be used as a vehicle for League racing.

11.1.5. The Code of Conduct applies to Hosted Sessions.

11.1.6. Violations of the Code of Conduct may be protested in accordance with Section 8. of this sporting code.

12. NASCAR Sanctioning

12.1. NASCAR Division will follow the F.I.R.S.T license progression requirement and the following series will constitute the NASCAR divisions. (See Table 11.1)

12.2. Points will be calculated in the same way as the FIRST-sanctioned series (Ref: Section 4.6) in all NASCAR Divisions with the exception of the Drivers World Championship.

12.3. The NASCAR Drivers World Championship will use the NASCAR-Sanctioned Points system without averaging.

12.4. Any driver leading a lap during the race will be awarded 5 bonus points with the driver leading the most laps of the race receiving an additional 5 bonus points. Counting the five-point bonuses available for leading at least one lap and leading the most laps, a race winner can earn a maximum of 195 points, creating a possible maximum of 25 points between first- and second-place finishers. (See Table 11.4)

12.5. All NASCAR Drivers World Championship Races will have at least one live Race Steward physically present during races.

12.6. NASCAR Competition Advisory Board

12.6.1. Members will include iRacing.com Staff and NASCAR Staff.

12.6.2. All appeals will be heard by the iRacing.com Appeals board which will contain at least one NASCAR official.

12.6.3. Appeals of penalties involving NASCAR Sanctioned events will be submitted to NASCAR.Appeal@iracing.com using the format as outlined in Section 9 of this document.

Table 12.1

License Class	Car/Series	Number of Weeks
Class D	Chevy Monte Carlo Late Model	Standard 12 Weeks
Class C	Chevy Silverado Truck	Standard 12 Weeks
Class B	Chevy Impala Class B	Standard 12 Weeks
Class A	Chevy Impala SS	Closely Follow Cup Series Feb Nov
Pro-Series	Chevy Impala SS/Pro-Series	See NASCAR Pro-Doc
Drivers World Championship	Chevy Impala SS/DWCS	See NASCAR Pro-Doc

Index

3D 12
accident recovery 45
AMD 4
anisotropic filtering 24
anti-aliasing 24
ATI 3, 4, 13, 24
ATI Eyefinity 3, 13
audio 6
baseline setup
    Skip Barber F2000 66
    Solstice 56
    Spec Racer Ford 61
Black Viper 8
blink 9
BlueTiger (motion cockpit) 14
Bluetooth 7
Bodnar (input components) 11, 12
BRD (wheel hardware) 10
BU0836 .... 11, See Bodnar (input components)
Buttkicker 14
button box 12
cable (internet) 9, 35, 109
car comparison 75
Carroll Smith 21, 24, 32
caster 24
Centripetal Circuit .... 100, See skidpad
Charlotte Motor Speedway 94, 95, 97, 98
chat 7, 21, 22, 30, 49, 102, 109, 124, 125, 127
ClubSport pedals 10
clutch 9, 10, 11, 40
clutch pedal 10
cockpit
    seat 6, 14, 17, 18, 19
cockpit designs 16
cockpit stability 17
Computer Parts Vendors 2
conceding 44
cooling (computer) 5, 16
CPU 4, 6, 16
Crossfire 3
CST (Cannon Simulation Technologies) .. 10, 11, 12
curbs 26, 30, 89
CXC Motion Simulators 14

damage modeling 12
data acquisition 20
data-logging 20
debrief 48
defending 42
DisplayPort 3, 13
Driftbox (telemetry file viewer) 20
drivers (computer system) 8
Driving Force GT (Logitech wheel) 9, 24
driving position 17
DSL 9, 35
ECCI (wheel hardware) 10
entry list 38
environment (sim racing) .... viii, 11, 13, 15, 16, 18, 103
ergonomics 15
eyestrain 16
Fanatec 9, 10, 16
FFB .... See Force Feedback
field of view 3
foot pain 17
footwear 17
Force Dynamics (motion simulators) 14
force feedback 24, 26
Force Feedback 9
forums 12, 16, 18, 20, 21, 22, 33, 34, 50, 102, 103, 124
FreeTrack 14
Frex (wheel hardware) 10
G25 .... 9, 11
G27 .... 9, 11
gamepad 12
gauge 12, 49
GPU (Graphics Processor) 3, 5, 16
graphics card 3, 4, 5, 8
grid 38
hard disk 5
head tracking 13
headphones 6
H-pattern shifter 11
humidity 16
input lag 11, 24
Intel 4

iRacing Dashboard	34
iSpeed	20, 36
Jefferson Circuit	91
keyboard	6, 7, 15, 18
gaming	7
knee pain	18
Laguna Seca	26, 27, 81, 82, 84
lapping	44
LCD shutter glasses	12
LEDs	12, 13, 14
lighting	15
Lime Rock Park	26, 27, 77, 78, 80
line conditioner	16
load cell	10, 11
Logitech	7, 10
memtest (RAM memory test)	4
microphone	7
Microsim MK II Racebase (DIY cockpit)	16
motherboard	3, 4, 5, 6, 19
motion cockpit	14
multiple monitor setup	12
NASCAR	128
network hardware	8
network latency	9
network speed test	9
Nixim mod (G25 brake modification)	11
nVidia	3, 4
Obutto	16, 19
operating system	7
paddle shifter	11
pedals	9, 10, 11, 15, 17, 18, 23, 25, 28, 31, 45, 98
ping	See network latency
Playseats	16
potentiometer	10, 11, 23
power supply	5, 6, 35
practice	36
prediction code	9
protesting	49
qualifying	21, 31, 37, 38, 110, 111, 124
quality of signal (QoS modem settings)	9
RAM	4, 5, 6, 7, 16
reset	46
router	8, 9, 35
safety rating	49
schedule	28, 34
sequential shifter	11

setup	30
default	31
stable	31
shift light indicator	12
Simboots	17
SimCraft (motion cockpits)	14
skidpad	24, 25, 100
Skip Barber F2000	viii, 26, 40, 62, 76
SLI (nVidia)	4, 12
slip angle	24
SoftTH	3, 13
Solstice	52
sound	See audio
Speakers	6
Spec Racer Ford	viii, 24, 40, 52, 57
split times	20, 24
Sporting Code	viii, 33, 45, 50, 101, 125
Version 2010.1.15.01	101
start	40
statistics	49
subwoofer	6, 15
Summit Point Raceway	26, 44, 85, 86, 88, 89, 91, 93
surge protector	16
telemetry	20
temperature	4, 16
TH2GO	3, 13
Thomas Superwheel (TSW)	10
time trial	37, 107
touchpad	6, 7, 18
trackball	7, 18
TrackIR	13, 14
transmission	10, 11, 40, 98
USB	5, 6, 7, 11, 12
vbox (telemetry data logger app)	20
visual distractions	15
voltage spikes	16
V-Sync	24
VW Jetta TDi	67
warm-up	39
wheel	9, 85
Windows 7	7
Windows Vista	7
Windows XP	6, 7
wireless	6, 7, 9
Xlerator	16

Final Thoughts

iRacing is only as fun as you make it. People who tend to be most frustrated are focused heavily on race-to-race changes in iRating and safety rating (SR). Safety rating is a measurement system that keeps people from causing wrecks and generally being difficult to race with. It relates to the number of corners you pass between incidents – corners per incident (CPI). If your CPI average goes down (more incidents than the average of your past several events), then your SR goes down, and vice versa. They add a 0.4 boost when you reach a whole number so that you don't gain and lose eligibility easily for a race series that requires a minimum SR. You lose that 0.4 when you go down past the same whole number.

In my experience, the most successful online sim racing leagues are those that emphasize clean racing, and for an open arrive-and-drive service it is clear that the safety rating system helps to reinforce this concept in all the drivers. And the importance of it is readily apparent when races are set up where the safety rating is not a factor … they are usually unpleasant and riddled with incidents.

Many complain about being "penalized" for another driver's mistakes or benign errors like dropping a wheel onto the grass. Well, first in order to record an incident for an off-track excursion, the middle of the car must be off the track – which would be rough on the equipment and somewhat more dangerous than keeping all four wheels on the track, and thus needs to have an incentive to stay "in bounds". For getting a 4x incident as a result of other driver's mistakes – well, that's racing. You have to deal with it, and hopefully learn from it because in many cases if you review the situation that led up to the incident, there may have been something you did which made the risk of an accident higher, even if you were not to blame. If you can learn to lessen the risk of not only your own driving mistakes and also lower the chances of having incidents with others, then you will go a long way in improving your skills and your enjoyment.

As well, it is important that both drivers have to suffer from a collision since it will make the driver who is principally to blame more aware of his mistake and be more likely to correct himself and never let it happen again. If I take someone out of a race due to my own poor skills, race decisions, or preparation, then the guilt and shame of not only bringing my own CPI down, but of the innocent driver as well, will go a long way in making me work harder to improve my racing ability. That is the whole point. Without that psychological incentive of limiting others 'pain' I would probably not learn from those mistakes and be more likely to repeat them.

Also, never compare your SR gain or loss to other drivers. If they are at a lower license level or a lower SR rating, they have a lower CPI and thus their resulting gain or loss of SR depends on if their CPI improves or worsens. It is like a batting average in baseball. Two people can go 2 for 5 and one can improve their average and the other may go down. The important thing is to focus on your own driving and trying to improve.

As for iRating, when you focus on driving and having fun, your iRating will eventually settle to your inherent skill level. If you work hard on improving your skills and maintain healthy safety habits, you will see improvements in your iRating. I recommend setting some realistic goals and work on the details and driving habits to reach them. Focusing on the minor ups and downs along the way will spoil the fun.

Printed in Great Britain
by Amazon